Ottakar's LOCAL HISTORY *Series*

Aberdeen

ANOTHER PRESE FROM FREDA.

OUR ANNIVERARY June 11" 2003

Aberdeen's maritime prosperity was based on fishing and ship-building.

Ottakar's LOCAL HISTORY *Series*

Aberdeen

Graeme Crowe

OTTAKAR'S

TEMPUS

First published 2002

Tempus Publishing Limited
The Mill, Brimscombe Port,
Stroud, Gloucestershire, GL5 2QG

© Ottakar's plc, 2002

British Library Cataloguing in Publication Data.
A catalogue record for this book is available from the British Library.

ISBN 0 7524 2663 x

Typesetting and origination by Tempus Publishing Limited
Printed in Great Britain by Midway Colour Print, Wiltshire

Contents

Acknowledgements   6

Introduction and Foreword   7

List of Contributors   8

1. Recollections   9

2. An Aberdeen Miscellaney   41

3. Aberdonian Allsorts   65

4. The Harbour at the
    Heart of the City   91

5. Wartime   109

6. The Past in the Present   119

Ship-building in the fifties. In slow decline until its eventual end in the nineties.

Acknowledgements

My biggest thanks, of course, go to all who took the time to contribute to this book. For all those who entered the competition and made the editing such an enjoyable experience, I'm sorry you weren't all successful.

Thanks to my colleagues at Ottakar's for allowing me the time required – and not grumbling about my absences from the front desk!

To Vicky Dawson for the encouragement and support.

To Claire Waldie and Laraine Waldie for helping me through the morass of e-mails and typing.

To Catherine Taylor and the staff of Aberdeen Central Library.

To Mike Day and Catherine Walker of Aberdeen Maritime Museum.

To Victoria Murchie of *The Press and Journal*.

And to Doris Davidson for her time and contributions.

Introduction

Aberdeen is a city rich in local history. There are many excellent, well-researched and beautifully written volumes about the city's past. How then to continue the interest in local history through this Ottakar's production? The happy answer is to give the people a chance to air their own memories and interests in their own words through the pages of this Tempus book. This is what I have tried to do in this volume. The only real difficulty has been in deciding what goes in and what stays out.

The essence of local history has, I hope, been distilled into this book; real people, telling it like it is (or was!). The myriad possibilities have been evident throughout the selection process, and it is obvious that these are just a glimpse of the many tales to be told.

Those selected display a wide range of subjects, interests and, above all, enthusiasm. Obviously, for all our dour image, we Aberdonian's like to communicate. Blethers? Certainly not! Keep reading, keep writing.

Graeme Crowe

Foreword

Bringing Aberdeen's more recent history to life will be a challenge for all involved in it. Cynics say that facts can't be changed, but each person who writes a story will have a different slant on what took place, perhaps making us view the event from another aspect altogether.

Born in a second floor tenement house in Rosemount, and having lived, worked and retired in the city, I have always been proud to call myself an Aberdonian, and I am certain that all writers of the pieces contained in this book feel the same as I do.

Surviving the ice-cold winters on the North Sea coast gives us resilience to criticism. Who amongst us really gets upset by jokes about our meanness, a fabrication which our forefathers encouraged to grow? We have so much to be proud of, and although many of our former industries have gone to the wall – granite, ship-building, glove and comb-making to name a few – we can still hold our heads high. Aberdeen is now regarded as the oil capital of Europe, with all the spin–offs that entails. Besides, we can still export men and women with brains, courage and artisitic talents to the rest of the world. What is more, many of those who left to find more lucrative work came back to their birthplace in retirement. They proved the truth of the city's motto: Happy to meet, sorry to part, happy to meet again.

BON ACCORD!
Good luck to this very worthwhile project.

Doris Davidson
Author of *Back of Beyond*.

List of Contributors

Bill Sutherland
Mary Munro
Winnie Carnegie
Lin Brown
George Anderson
Jacqueline Beattie
Innes Murchie
Doris Davidson
Gordon Casely
E. Davidson
Pamela Tate
Alan Morrice
Lizzie Finlayson
David Tallach

R.J. Arthur
John W. Mathieson
J. Trevor Jenkins
Peter Jones
Anders Ingram
Andy Duff
Peter Myers
Vic Gibson
Gordon Bathgate
William Watt
Derek Fraser
Olive Walterson
Kerry J. Morrison

1 Recollections

Poverty and providence

Growing up during the great depression provided a harsh, austere background for childhood. These days formed in everyone a basic instinct and ability to survive. When working, father was an ironsmith in the shipyards, only at that time there was no work, year upon year. The allowance from the 'Bureau' (Buroo) left little or nothing for food after the demands of such items as rent, gas and electricity. The deficiency was real, life threatening and I hope what follows gives some idea of the desperate battle most were engaged in for survival.

Mother had an old treadle sewing machine that had belonged to her mother; it proved to be a godsend. Those who had an income from some menial task were immeasurably better off than the totally unemployed. Women would come to mother with one of their old coats. How often have I heard the question, 'Can you make a pair of breeks for Andrew/Billy/Tommy or whoever?' Mother had made brown paper patterns of the shapes required to be cut from the old coats. She would try them this way and that to see if enough material was contained in the old garment to make a pair of breeks, the short trousers worn by the boys of the day. She would spend hours marking, cutting, and sewing. First the cloth, then the material for the lining. Button holes for the fly were laboriously cut, formed and hand stitched. The old button box was raided again and again

to provide a matching set of buttons. Linings were sewn in place, and careful ironing followed to provide a quality finish.

The work would take about a week as mother tried to find time from scrubbing, washing, knitting and cleaning to provide for father and her own three boys. Oh yes, she also went to the west end three days a week to skivvy for some 'toff's' family for a pittance – twelve and a half pence – walking both ways to save the tram fare. By the way, for the trousers she so painstakingly made, she received six pence – two and a half pence in today's currency.

Oatmeal was a great standby. Porridge in the morning, often without milk, and for dinner and tea. Money was eked out penny by penny from 'Buroo' day, Friday, and was usually all gone by Monday night. So what was to be done? Some of the few well off could be seen in their leisure pursuit on the golf course, so father, my brothers and myself would keep out of the way of the players (for the law of trespass applied) and comb the rough grass for golf balls. Those found would be taken home, washed and cuts repaired with a hot knife. They were then sold back to the sportsmen for a penny or halfpenny depending on condition.

Many days were spent fishing in the sea. This had nothing to do with pleasure but was born of necessity. Catches of cod, mackerel and whiting, were worth their weight in gold. The mouth of the Don also provided some fish, but by and large was not so productive.

The Ben Screel *aground at Nigg Bay. (Aberdeen Art Gallery and Museums Collection)*

Elder brother George would be up at first light on Saturdays and Sundays and walk all the way to Hazlehead, for before the advent of caddie cars, older boys were in demand as caddies to carry the clubs of 'gentleman' players. Sometimes George would be round twice in a day, walk home, hand the money he'd earned over to mother, then fall fast asleep with exhaustion. I was, and still am, particularly proud of my elder brother. I remember he won a bursary to attend the Central school. Clothing and boots were sometimes supplied by local councils, for poorer families, after a degrading means test. These items were easily recognisable by their colouring and general ugliness. The stigma of wearing them was terrible. George attended the 'Central' so clothed, and, being extremely intelligent and sensitive, felt the shame that was none of his making. Human nature being what it is, some teachers and pupils looked disdainfully upon him. George gave them all the best answer – Dux of the school! What an answer to the ignorant.

As a boy I also remember seeing the beach links covered by a pendulous, frosty fog suspended two or three feet above the grass. Wisps of fog detaching from the main body would swoop gracefully down to form 'stalagmites' that seemed to support the main blanket. In a shallow bank of this mist, the odd hardy soul out for their constitutional walk would appear almost as spectres; their heads moving above the blanket of fog while their legs seemed to move independently, below.

One particularly fierce winter, it could have been the year that the *Ben Screel* floundered on the rocks of Nigg bay, a combination of gales and tides produced a phenomenon that I have never seen since. The sea was whipped into a cauldron. Foam and spume were flung right over the promenade to cover the golf links in a shivering jelly-like mass. The tidal limits were broken by the sea and the water streamed through the bridge by the salmon fisher's bothy, covering the links. The spume blanket waltzed weirdly on the flooded surface.

In the winter when streets were thick with snow, the unemployed were given the task of hand-clearing this, shovel by shovel. Forced out in the worst of weather, they were ill-shod

and poorly clothed. Many times my father suffered from bronchitis as a consequence.

Our humble abode had a fireplace, but this was of little use without fuel, which was priced out of reach, but necessity is the mother of invention. Imagine a house facing directly into a north-east gale blowing off the North Sea. The living room of the house is draughty, damp, sparsely furnished and very cold. Such was our abode. Pleurisy and bronchitis were common ailments in the lower social order to which we were confined. So how to survive? At the bottom of School Road, near the Aulton Links, there was and is a spread of football pitches. These of my youth differed from today's in that they were covered with cinders as a playing surface – just about the most foolish practice imaginable – yet this was common at the time. The cuts and grazes

Shovelling snow was a money earner. (Aberdeen Art Gallery and Museums Collection)

Aberdeen beach – a beachcomber's paradise?

sustained when players fell on these sharp cinders were terrible. Any of the old players surviving have black patches showing under the skin of their knees and elbows as a result of falls in their youth. Whatever the absurdity of cinders for this purpose, we turned the 'foolishness of men' into the means of our survival.

The cinders that covered the football pitches had to be constantly replaced as they disintegrated and were blown away by the high winds. At that time, Aberdeen town gas was made in the retorts at Cotton Street by the way of burning coal and gathering the escaping gas into the gas holder. The coal reaches a point where most of the gas is extracted, then the residual coke is ejected into steel wagons and cooled. The coke thus formed was sold as cinders for domestic use. It was also used to cover the playing surfaces of the football pitches of the day.

We would watch from our living room window for the lorries that shuttled the coke from the gas works to dump them in a huge pile alongside the football pitches at the bottom of School Road. As soon as a new load was dumped, an army of freezing scavengers would descend on this prey with an assortment of old prams and 'cairties.' By dint of careful selection and painful picking with numb fingers, the assorted vehicles would be gradually filled with cinders and used as fuel in our fireplace. My brothers and I were of this fraternity, born of want.

Through George's ingenuity we stole a march on the other gleaners. He found that if we filled a basin with water and poured a shovel-full of the waste into the water, the unusable clinker sank and the fireworthy cinder floated. Before long we had the fuel cellar filled to the roof. The fireplace glowed with a welcoming glowing warmth. The whole of life seemed to change with that one fire.

It's funny how one man's misfortune can turn out to benefit another. Such was the case

one winter day as we as a family were beach-combing. It was apparent that the storm had washed the deck cargo from some ship. The seashore was littered with railway sleepers, all soaked in creosote to prevent them rotting. Immediately a recovery operation swung into being to retrieve them. The faithfull 'cairtie' mobilised, we ran to the beach, father, George, Ron and myself. So heavy were these sleepers that we could take only one at a time as the wheels of our transport sank in the sands. However with a combination of perspiration and inspiration we trailed them home into our basement cellar time after time. An old crosscut saw and much elbow grease produced a wonderful store of potential warmth, as the mountain of 'cloggies' grew. We were never in any doubt that some higher providence was always at work on our behalf, such was the constant provision for our needs in the most unlikely manner.

A penny was a lot of money in these days. This is why it was George entrusted with one of our few pennies that day to purchase a penny packet of tea. Ron and he were running through the puddles and melting snow to reach the shop, then disaster! The penny flew out of George's hand and disappeared. They stood dumb struck. 'The penny's gone,' George wailed. Ron thought he detected a dying movement in the water about ten feet away. With numb fingers they fished in the freezing murk. A minute turned to five, ten. 'Oh gosh, it looks hopeless.' Ron was despairing but they searched on. 'Ooh!' George's eyes lit up 'Here's something.' He fumbled in the water. Awkwardly he grasped the hidden thing, fighting the numbness. 'Look!' He withdrew his hand. He pointed with his left index finger. Pinned against the back of the penny by his frozen thumb was a gleaming silver sixpenny piece. God indeed works in mysterious ways, His wonders to perform!

On another stormy day during his 'beat' along the seashore, dad was halfway between the beach access bridge and the mouth of the Don. His walk had thrown up nothing of use and he was rather despondent. As the breakers crashed on the beach and receded with their familiar hissing sound, they could have been mocking his predicament, but then again; maybe they were drawing his attention! As one particular breaker crashed and receded, a flapping movement caught his eye. Oblivious to the discomfort, he dashed into the shallows and snatched at a proffered lashing tail. Yanking upwards, he couldn't believe his eyes. A seven-pound salmon had been deposited on the beach for his taking! I knew nothing about it until, on rising from bed that winter morning, he said 'Go and look in the sink Bill, I caught a sardine today'. With the innocence of a child I went to look. I was amazed. This beautiful silver fish was curled at its head and tail because the sink could not contain it.

Brother Ron was a great searcher and finder, so much so dad accorded him the honourable title of 'Ronnie the raik'. It was amazing how he found things. Walking with him one day on our way to school, he suddenly bounded forward and lifted a piece of paper from the ground, a ten-shilling note! All grist to the mill of our survival. That was the wonderful thing, nothing was kept to oneself, everything was handed to mum as contributing to the common good. He had somehow worked out that at bends in the river Don below a bridge, anything that was lost or thrown over was carried by the current to that particular spot. He reasoned with uncanny accuracy and was constantly rewarded in his searching at these places.

The highlight of his finding career though, was the time we were searching a tip on the sight of where the Chris Anderson sports stadium now stands. It had produced many convertible treasures over the years but none better than the one we found that day. After a short spell digging, Ron came upon a blue metal box measuring some eight inches by four or three. It was heavy, dirty and tightly closed. We washed it in a nearby burn and, after a struggle, prised the lid open. Lo and behold – a veritable treasure trove of foreign coins. Dad consulted some of his cronies with some knowledge of numismatics then took the coins to an accredited dealer, I don't remember the exact sum it produced but I think it was in the region of twelve pounds – ten weeks income on our grand scale.

George left school on obtaining a good office job with a cattle society. Dad found work as shipbuilding revived. The grip of poverty gradually eased and we moved house. Ron found a job and then it was my turn. Mother said she had never been so well off. That was true of all of us.

The lessons that we learned, the exercises in survival, often formed the subject of our discussions years afterwards, and we traced the hand of providence working time and again on our behalf through these strenuous times.

Bill Sutherland

Halloween
Prize Winning Entry

I've aye liket Halloween! Maybe, lang syne, in anither life I wis a wizened auld witch fa enjoyed aa the shenanigans o Halloween nicht, afore cooryin doon tae hide awa the neist day. Aye, maybe I hiv a gweed jelp o heathen bleed, for richt fae the time I wis a bairn, I've aye hid thon belly-grippin feelin as October days grow short, an the time for ghoulies an ghaisties comes roon again.

We rakit the glory hole, an mam's auld rag bag for weeks afore. 'Fit are ye gaun as, at Halloween?' ye'd be speired at the squeel. 'I'm nae tellin' cam the answer, as sure as faith. Warm drawers under granny's jet-beaded frock wis a good notion, as the nicht could be cauld like death itsel. There wis thon tartan shawl that mither eesed tae weir roon her shooders fan she hid the flu – that wid dae fine wi a fause face wi a lang plooky nose an a pinted chin.

'Gweed be here,' I thocht wi a smyrk as I tried on the auld braws ae nicht. 'Fit a ticket. I jist need tae mak some hair that looks like cats' sookins an I wid fleg onybody I meet!' The day afore, we daundered doon the Tullich road, jist as innocent as a lammye. Quick as a wink, in ower the palin, alang the neep dreels we crept, lookin for the richt neep. The bashed tattie bogle squinted at ye wi his gley een, bit niver said a word. As seen as I found a neep that wis even-like, an nae shargert or wizzent, in unner the oxters o my jaicket I plunkit it, an oot the road we went, the dubby neep filin my gweed school claes aneth my jaicket.

Aince the lamp wis kinnelt, an the wax cloth wis back on the table, faither wad gie me a haun tae scoop oot the hard bits o the neep. Ye didna wint a foggy neep – they didna taste gweed, for it wis fine tae chaw some o the juicy, yalla neep as we worked awa.

There wis a fine smell tae, a bit like the smell o warm foamy milk an sharny-tailed coos munchin their sliced-up yalla neeps. Aince ye'd scooped it oot, ye made its physog as coorse an frichtsome as ye could manage; big tuskers o teeth an bleed comyn oer the jaw, a nose oot o a carrot, an gless bools for the een. Wool wippit roon the lid made a gweed heid o hair.

Guisers.

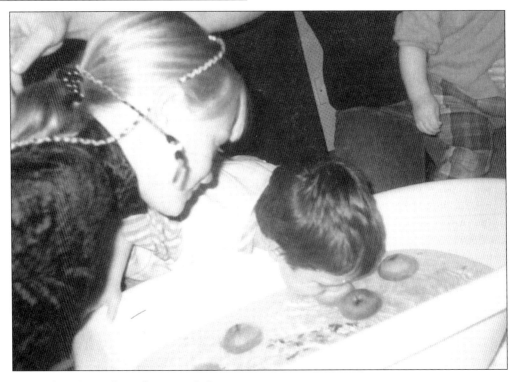

Dookin for apples – still a Halloween standard.

Fin aa wis said an deen, I wis fair tricket wi this year's neep lantern. There wis a look o Auntie Nellie aboot the face. Faiher aye said she hid a face that minded him o a neepie lantern! A bit o caunle, a length o binder twine, an it wis deen. Halloween nicht could come noo fan it likit, for I wis ready.

Halloween that ae year I mine o, wis cauld, the kin o cauld that jeers yer bleed. As the dark crept doon, so did the frost, snell and keen. Aifter my tea, that I could hardly swalla for excitement, I dressed up in my Halloween gear, fine an warm, kinnelt my lantern, an set off doon the walkie tae meet twa or three o my cronies.

Lauch an cairry-on we aa hid, as we fingered ane anithers' ferlies, claes fae auld kists that hidna seen the licht o day for fifty year, auld beets trailed oot fae the wash hoose press. Aabody hid a neep, some fae the gairden, an some snaffled like oor een fae the

fairmer's park doon the road side. They'd aa spent a lang forenicht howkin their lanterns as best they could.

Aff we set on oor roons. It wis jist an unwritten law that ye stuck tae yer ain streets. Ye niver thocht o poachin on ither bairns' territories, bit we seen heard them, bourachs o bairns, riggit oot like oorsels, lauchin an kecklin as they trauchled alang in trailin frocks an beets that didna fit.

'We'll ging tae Jessie Johnstons first. She aye gings tae her bed at seven an, forbye, she aye gies ye a gweed haunfu o sweeties an a saxpence as weel!' suggested ae body. Jessie wis waitin for her guisers. She wid hae been fair doon-hertit gin we hidna geen her a knock.

'Ony Halloween?' wis the cry, as her reed slorach o a face beamed at us fae the porch. 'Ye'll need tae dee a turn for me first,' she wheezled, so we trotted oot the feel jokes as rhymes, an sang yon sappy song aboot a wifie on a rock in Germany. We'd learnt it fae the singin wifie last week, an we thocht it wis a bit gleckit, bit Jessie thocht it wis awfu bonny an haunded oer oor sweeties an things withoot a myowt.

'Awa ye go noo ye limmers, an dinna wauken the wife doon the road. She's near eneuch at death's door so she winna wint you lot rappin at her door the nicht.

As we passed a road end, twa or three geets shout 'Ging doon tae Mrs Henderson's. She's makin CHIPS an ye get them in a real paper pyoke!'

Aff we raced tae Aggie Henderson's, an sure eneuch, there wis a line o bairns at her back door. The windae in the scullery wis wide tae the waa, an the sweet hum o fat an fryin tatties made yer wame turn ower. We waited oor turn, hopin the tatties widna rin oot, or the chip pan ging up in a bleeze afore we got oor chips.

Seen aifter we'd said oor bitties tae Aggie, we fairly got a poke o bilin het chips, lathered in salt an vinegar. Fit rare they tasted in the frosty nicht air, wi oor het breith makin a myst fan ye opened yer moo! That wis the best we iver hid! But we did the roons, even the Bobby's hoose. Fan he came tae the door wi his carpets an his galluses on, michty me, he looked like ony ither mannie withoot his uniform an his helmet. An for aince, he forgot foo, only a wikk back, he'd catched us in Lang Tam's gairden pinchin his soor aipples.

He wis near eneuch human that nicht o Halloween, an he lauched an joked in thon hoarse wey he hid, as tho he'd a buckie stuck in his thrapple.

'Get aff the streets by nine o clock or I'll skelp yer docks for ye!' wis his send aff tae us, bit we jist gied a lauch an left him on the doorstep. He was grinnin like an ape an

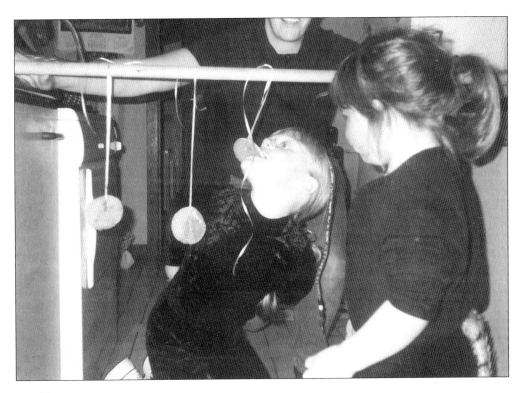

...and jammy scones

mindin fine o the nichts fan he hid deen the same as a bairn, an nae hairm taen.

Mam's auld patchwirk bag wi the cane haunles wis getting real heavy as we wandered on, knockin an singin like linties, till seen oor throats were dry an sair. That wifie in The Buildings maun hae been a witch, for she kent that we needed a drink o lemonade tae help us on oor road. The bag jingled an knappit against oor happit legs. Seen, we'd deen the hale street.

There wis a special feel aboot that nicht – as though somethin coorse an horrible micht jist loup oot at ye roon a corner. We bade in twas an threes, jist in case! Lang efter half echt, fair founert, we left ane anither tae trail hame. Aince in the hoose, my lantern, lang oot an smelling foosty wi its burnt neep smell, wis left in the porch tae be thrown oot tae the scaffie the morn's mornin. Aa the auld claes cam aff in a flash, an wi dirlin fingers I teemed oot my bag.

We were greedy deevils bit it did yer hert gweed tae see aa the tangerines, aipples, toffee, granny's sookers, nuts, wine gums an even a 'sair heidie' wrapped in a paper hunky, spread oot on a rag rug afore the fire. Ye coonted yer pennies an saxpences like Mydas wi his siller. 'Ten shillins an saxpence... I bet that's mair than Jock got next door!' Aa ye got fae mam wis a gentle scud on the lug tae get ye tae the sink tae sweel yer hauns an face, for there wis squeel the morn.

So that wis Halloween for anither year, bit it wis rare fun I thocht, as I drifted aff tae sleep, maybe tae dream o aa the ghaists an creepy things ye could hae met in the darkened nicht streets. 'I div believe in witches an ghosties,' I murmer tae masel as my een close, 'or else there widna be a Halloween!'

Mary Munro

A happy summer holiday

Back in the 1920s and '30s not many people had a holiday. I was one of the lucky ones, because each summer my mother, sister and brother had a week in Aberdeen staying with my grannie and my aunt. My dad could never come, as he wasn't allowed any time off his work, with long hours slaving in an office in Peterhead. We lived three miles out at Inverugie, and it was from there that we caught the puffing train to Aberdeen.

My auntie, Maggie Mitchell, was a teacher at the Normal School all her working days. She was my mother's sister, and being the oldest daughter in a family of nine, it was her duty to stay at home and support her widowed mother. Later on, two invalid brothers, wounded and shell-shocked from the First World War, also required her care. Thus, she had to sacrifice her own future happiness. She had the same 'young man' all her days until they both died in their late seventies. We knew about her romance, for he called once a week and the two of them went out for a walk along Westburn Drive where she lived. Just a few houses away from my grannie's was open countryside. We'd peep at them from the top bedroom window and wait for the magic moment when he took her arm. 'Lad and lass,' we'd shout among ourselves, and were immediately rebuked by our mother.

All nine, when young in the 1880s and '90s, had in turn been pupils at the Normal School. It was fee-paying then, with a reduction for each child in the family, so that by the time the youngest started, she went free. But times change, and when my auntie was a teacher there, the pupils mainly came from very poor homes. After the summer holidays, on return to school, she used to ask if anyone had had a holiday. Up shot a few hands, and the commonest answer was, 'We had a picnic in the Trainie Gardens' and sometimes an afternoon at the Sea Beach. One small boy

Walking out.

excelled himself by reporting that his father had given him a penny all to himself, as he'd spent his holidays collecting 'horse's oranges' from the street. No doubt his dad flogged them to anyone lucky enough to have a garden. Needless to say, the Normal School has long since closed, and I don't even know if the building still stands.

We had many exciting outings, mostly on foot, to the Westburn Park or the Duthie Park, but on a really sunny day, we'd pay a half penny on a green tramcar with an open roof and go to the Sea Beach. Sometimes we went in the opposite direction into the country, this time on a red tramcar – again a halfpenny fare and an open roof, but its terminus was the Bieldside Inn. We'd walk down to the river Dee and admire all the wild flowers growing on the banks.

Maybe our favourite and most exciting expedition to faraway places was when we went on a charabanc ride. The fleet of charabancs stood in the Castlegate, each with a blackboard in front, their destinations written in white chalk. One was called 'A Mystery Tour' which we thought about, then decided to have a circular tour instead, first to Stonehaven, then Banchory and home via Culter and Cults.

The charabancs were like big open buses, four or five to a seat, with the driver pointing out places of interest. We decided to avoid the 'Mystery Tour', because we had heard about a Peterhead worthy who had read about these

On the beach at Stonehaven.

charabancs and was very keen to get through to Aberdeen to see what they really looked like. He saved and saved for many months until he had enough money to pay his bus fare to Aberdeen. From the terminus in Mealmarket Street he rushed up to the Castlegate and there they were, rows and rows of them. He had never heard of most of the places they were going to, Aboyne, Ballater, Alford etc. – all unknown to him.

He settled for the 'Mystery Tour' and with great excitement took his seat, the big day he had looked forward to for so long had really arrived. The charabanc headed out of King Street, over the Bridge of Don, and alas, carried on the North turnpike through Balmedie and Ellon with the driver pointing out the places our passenger knew so well.

Have you guessed his fate? The first stop was outside Peterhead Prison where they watched some convicts at work, then on to the Blue Toon itself to stop in Broad Street outside 'the conveniences' with an hour to spare to look around the shops or have a cup of tea. He had told his friends so much about his planned outing, that to bump into any of them would have caused such a laugh. So it was a quick walk for him down side streets before sliding in to sit in the charabanc until it was time to leave. Back to Aberdeen, he had just enough time to run to catch his bus to Peterhead. News soon leaked out of his plight, and there were many giggles among his friends.

But, to get back to our happy day out, we boarded the charabanc and followed the coast road to Stonehaven, where we stopped at the sea front to let us look at this new view of the sea and to gaze at all the strangers strolling along the promenade in the summer sunshine. The charabanc went slowly through the town, where we could glance at the shops in passing, and the driver announced we were going to Banchory via the Slug Road. We were sitting just behind him and he turned to my young brother and told him that when the road was being built, the workmen ran out of stones and used dead slugs instead. We believed him!

Our next stop was on the Brig o'Feugh, where we were told to admire the falls and see if we could spot any salmon leaping. Again, the helpful driver turned his head and asked me this time if I could spell 'Feugh'.

'Well, I'll tell you,' he added, 'it's F, U, ECH, ECH – Feugh'. I believed him, thinking we are a long, long way from our little country school at Tortorston, so they must have a different alphabet here. We certainly didn't have the letter 'ECH' in our vocabulary.

We had time in Banchory to have a delicious slider from D'Agostinos, the very good Italian ice cream shop, and a cup of tea for the adults, as well as a look round the unknown shops. The charabanc sat in the High Street waiting for us all to return at the appointed hour, and then we turned towards home, following the beautiful Dee Valley. Our next stop was on the bridge at Culter where the driver pointed out the huge wooden statue of Rob Roy standing so majestically, brightly painted and holding a sword. He gazed at us from a high rock overlooking the Culter Burn. The driver told us how that brave man had leapt across the water from the rock to escape his enemies. I can still remember – with fear – the wild look in his eyes and how tall he was. On we went

Brig o' Feugh.

through Bieldside and Cults, where we met a red tramcar. We had been on it the day before to stand on the Shakkin' Briggie at Cults and make it shak!

What a delightful and exciting day we'd had, and as we returned to the Castlegate, we were now longing to get home in the tram to tell Grannie about all the faraway and wonderful places we had seen, and how we'd driven along a road that was built of dead slugs.

Winnie Carnegie
Illustrations by Lin Brown

The polony years
Prize Winning Entry

We shared No. 55 Charlotte Street with three other council tenants. For twenty years we lived in continuous peace and harmony (if you don't count fistfights of less than fifteen minutes and the pitched battle on the drying green in 1968). Now it's possible that Charlie Yule who lived in the sunks, or the Stewarts who lived in the attic, sat down of an evening to chargrilled sea bream with cous-cous and rocket salad, but my guess is what we ate, they ate. Likewise in a thousand working-class homes across the granite city in the early sixties.

Rationing ended the year I was born. Given the amount I could eat, no one was more willing to turn the coupons to confetti than Ma Anderson.

Breakfast consisted of dough in the guise of the Aberdeen roll. For a decade I ate two rolls a day. That's 7,300 all told. Mental arithmetic buffs will already have calculated that 7,300 rolls at two ounces per roll comes to sixty-five stone, or thirteen times my own body weight in dough by the time I was twelve. And remember, I'm not talking about dough with assorted nuts, dough with mung beans or dough with Shippam's multi-vitamin spread. I'm talking about dough – end of story.

During hard times (when the chancellor put tuppence on a pint for example) our roll ration was slashed. Some mornings, ma could afford only two rolls. The mathematical strain of dividing two lumps of dough into three equal parts (one for each of her sons) was often too much for her and she'd throw her slide-rule at the cat.

At school we were treated to the nutritional marvel of the age: milk. Government food fascists hell-bent on strengthening the nation's bones, insisted that all primary school children drank a third of a pint of milk a day. If you were lucky this wouldn't be enough to spoil your appetite for a Lucky Tattie at playtime. A Lucky Tattie was a hockey puck-sized slab of boiled sugar coated with cinnamon. Inside every tattie a plastic charm had been hidden. Lucky Tatties were so named because you were lucky if you had any fillings left after you'd chewed one.

At playtime we bought penny icicles, nutritious as snow. Once, to the great delight of the whole school, two shops across the road from the school engaged in an icicle war. The first shots were fired when one shop reduced their penny icicles to a halfpenny.

'How much are yer penny icicles mister?'

'A ha'penny loon.'

'I'll tak' a tanner's worth then.'

In a classic example of free-market economics, the other shop also dropped the price of their penny icicles to a halfpenny but added more flavours to each icicle. The first shop responded in kind, and so the war continued. They couldn't keep this up forever of course, but for a glorious spell in the summer of '63 you could buy, for a farthing, an icicle that had forty-eight flavours.

After school hunger pangs were warded off with pieces 'n' jam. The jam was made from equal measures by weight of neeps and sugar. This was spread thick on white bread from which all nutrients had been systematically thrashed at a secret location outside Kemnay.

We had the main meal of the day in the evening. This was often polony, the staple food of our childhood. Cut into slices, polony sausage could be grilled, fried, or used to wedge open doors. It had the nutritional value of pencil shavings. Ma bought it by the yard from the Home & Colonial on George Street. Recently, more than thirty years after sinking my gnashers into my first slice, I paused to read the food label on a polony sausage in the food hall of my local supermarket. The list of ingredients read like a script for *The Outer Limits*. After a harmless enough start (bacon, pork) came 'other meats'. *Which* other meats? Yak? Three-banded armadillo? Vulture? Next up, rusk. This is a kind of edible sawdust the government allows butchers to mix with meat while the customer is rooting in the veggie basket for a decent neep. At this point the print got so small I had to climb into Tesco's fridge to read it. On closer examination I noted with horror a telephone directory of E numbers.

By this time a hundredweight of oven chips had welded themselves to my shins, but it was the sudden realisation that we ate polony for *ten* years that chilled me to the bone.

There must have been a cave-in at the polony mine one year because I remember other meals. Mince and tatties with mealie puddings and doughballs, for instance. A doughball, as domestic scientists among you will already know, was a ball of dough. Fifteen minutes before you planned to eat, the doughballs were dropped into the hot mince like depth charges. Mealie puddings are bullets of meal and fat injected into a sausage skin.

The drill for supper was the same each night. Ma would gingerly set three plates of food on the table then dive behind the settee shouting 'supper!' A millisecond later all three brothers would arrive, frantically trying to calculate which plate contained most food before making a grab for it. James could count the peas on a plate at a single glance. In the stramash that inevitably followed, mince often landed on the roof.

When ma was working late at the Rainbow Café on Bridge Street, da made supper. Years before the phrase was coined, da invented fast food; it was fast because if he wasn't in the Crag by seven o'clock exactly, he'd never again lay a domino with pride. In 1963 the *Cragshannoch* dominoes team found out that Da sometimes made toad-in-the-hole and they sent him a white feather in the post.

On special occasions, like Bonnie Prince Charlie's birthday for example, we'd have pudding after supper. Usually semolina or bread and butter pudding, but sometimes Ma made jelly in a rabbit-shaped mould. God knows where she got the mould from. It probably came with the house. 'Here are the keys to the property, Mrs Anderson, and here's your rabbit-shaped jelly mould. We hope you will be happy as an Aberdeen Council tenant'.

Once a year we had chipped (pronounced 'chippit') fruit from The Orchard in Upperkirkgate. Chipped fruit was made up of all the fruit the fruiterer couldn't get away with selling to anybody sober: grapes that had been knelt on, oranges that had rolled under the wheels of a bus, bananas that had been used to hold the front door of the shop open, and so on. You could get a tea chest of chippit fruit for five bob.

Each of us had a favourite food. Ma was daft about cheese and jam sandwiches. Da's favourites were all fishy: cod roe (raans), buckies and crabs (he even liked Gerry Anderson's *Stingray* because it was set underwater). James had fallen in love with pomegranates. You'd need to have one flown in specially from Athens then so who knows where *he* got them. He'd sit for hours poking at the seeds with a pin.

I didn't like pomegranates or fish eggs. But I was foolish enough to try my hand at two recipes I got from my Grunny. The first was 'Black Sugar Ale' which sounded like something Long John Silver might have drunk. If he did he was as stupid as he looked. The penny should have dropped when I realised that the only place you could get the main ingredient was from a qualified chemist. From a chemist on George Street I bought a bullet of liquorice so concentrated it could only have been made at Dounreay. I had to sign a book before the chemist would hand it over. When I got home I put the slug of liquorice in an empty Hays Dazzle bottle and filled it with water and that was that. A simple recipe really. Grunny Anderson said 'Black Sugar Ale' improved with age, so I left it in the coal cellar for six weeks. The result was an anthracite-coloured sludge of extraordinary laxative power. After my first scoof they were sliding polony under the lavvy door for days.

I should have learned a lesson at this point. Instead I tried the second of Grunny Anderson's recipes – Olde Fashioned Lemonade. Seduced by the romantic allure of the concoction's title I gave it a go. I forget the details but it involved real lemons and a pair of Aunt Mary's tights. I couldn't bring myself to try the finished product.

Ma undertook twice nightly raids on Da's breeks; once in the early evening as Da slept off lunchtime's quota of Eighty Shilling ale, and again when he returned from the Cragshannoch after last orders. Loose change from these dangerous missions paid for pre-bedtime treats.

A typical early raid might net enough for 'ice cream and ale': a glass of lemonade (sugar, water and flavourings) and a scoop of ice cream (sugar, water, flavourings and fat). We'd all huddle around the coal fire watching *What's My Line?*, trying not to make too much noise with our spoons, and praying Da wouldn't wake up and audit his trousers.

The financial success of later raids depended on how lucky Da had been at three card brag. Most often the killer hand eluded him, but occasionally he'd sway home carrying enough coin to cripple a munitions pony and that meant chips for all!

There were two local chip shops: the Peppercorn in George Street and Archies in John Street. Archie fried everything in lard. Some evenings when the call of 'waiting on chips' had gone up and conversation faded, you could stand in the queue of regulars and listen to their arteries harden. Archies sold a liver and bacon slice: food of the Gods. The Peppercorn gave away anything left unsold at closing time and we were quick to take advantage of this. Just before closing time each night, Ma would send James to the Peppercorn wearing an empty rucksack. James had memorised his lines:

A pickled onion supper please, Martin. Just a half portion of chips tonight though please, that's all we can afford thank you very much. Ma has been thinking about selling Geoff to the gypsies if things don't get much better…

James usually staggered home with enough white puddings on his back to see us through the winter. Eventually Martin twigged and we had to take the padlock off the polony bunker again.

I once had a nightmare after a gargantuan meal of polony, mashed tatties, and neep jam. A vitamin had somehow managed to get into our house through a crack in the pointing and Da was chasing it around the living room, crashing off the cooker, falling over the settee, trying to kill it with the tattie masher.

They say you are what you eat. What a terrifying thought

George Anderson

Cairties, dazzies and delicious coo candy

I came to live in Don Street, Woodside, in 1953 at the age of five and spent the next seven years there in a happy, close community. The street had a row of terraced granite cottages on one side, where I lived, and opposite granite tenements, which were badly affected with subsidence. The subsidence was so bad in a friend's house that we raced cars down one end of the floor to the other whilst the dining table was propped at one end by books to keep food and drinks from spilling. The houses at each side of the street accommodated families in two and three rooms. The back gardens (backies) housed shared toilets, rows of coal cellars, tiny vegetable gardens and wash houses with drying greens (greenies) and two air raid shelters.

At the top of Don Street just opposite the Woodside Fountain was Strathdee's Bakery, nicknamed the Auld Breader because on a Saturday they sold bread and cakes that were left over from their shops, queues would form down the street while women bought up cheaply bags full of bashed cakes, bread and rolls by the dozen. Grannie would send me over with a shilling to get tipsy cakes which she made into delicious trifles that would be eaten as the family gathered on Saturday at her house for tea after the men returned from the football match. We would get pennies from our uncles and head off to buy gob stoppers, sherbet dips, penny caramels or a bar of coo candy, so named because of the picture of a highland cow on the wrapper. On return the radio would go on for the Scottish dance music and the rugs were rolled back as we danced round the room to a Scottish Waltz or the Gay Gordons. When the dancing finished

Don Street.

The backie.

we would wind up the gramophone and play Mario Lanza, Elvis Presley and Jimmy Shand records, often accompanied by a singsong.

At the end of the street was a blacksmith (smiddy) shop, where we were permitted to watch horses being shod. We stood entranced as we watched the fearsome, dark, muscular smiddy, clad in leathers, making the hammer sing as it shaped the red hot horseshoe against the anvil. Pleased with the shape of the shoe he would plunge it, spitting and hissing, into the cooling trough before nailing it to the hoof of the horse. Among his customers was Bobby, a large carthorse who came from the nearby Buckie Farm, along with his owner Mr Gordon who delivered fresh vegetables to almost every street in Woodside. Mr Gordon would blow a whistle to announce his arrival, but Bobby would announce his arrival at my

grannie's by scraping the pavement and neighing impatiently until we fetched him his customary piece.

He stubbornly refused to pass her house until he got his treat. Bobby in return would award us by lowering his head to be stroked and kissed and then allow us to climb aboard the cart for a hurl to the end of the street.

Just down from the smiddy was a railway bridge (briggie) and the shout would go out when a steam train was due. We ran to the briggie in time for the train to pass under and cover us with huge clouds of steam, causing us to shriek with laughter and cling to one another, blinded temporarily until the air cleared and we emerged all damp and full of glee at this wonderful experience.

Sometimes we rose early in the holidays and would sit quietly on the windowsill watching the day unfold. A trawler-man, heading home with the familiar rum-fuelled gait, came towards us with coppers for a sweetie. We accepted the money and he said that it would bring him luck at sea. Occasionally, cars passed at the head of the street along with the trains that squealed, screeched and threw sparks from the cables as they halted at the Woodside Fountain, allowing the droves of mill workers to alight on their way to work. The workers hurried down the street to the sound of the hooters (old wartime sirens) at the nearby Donside papermill and Grandholm woollenmill, beckoning them to work and later signalling the end of their working day. The hooters became our timepieces in the years that followed, calling us to the breakfast table, and, later in the day, signalling end of play as we rushed home for tea, as we knew lateness would not be excused.

Time was spent mostly making our own fun, and often playing games that had been handed down from our parents. 'Beddies', more commonly known as hopscotch, was played on the pavement. All we needed was a piece of broken slate to write the numbers on each slab, and a small pebble to throw as our marker. All the girls had skipping ropes (often cut from an old washing line) and sang various rhythmic songs and chants as they skipped. As we became more experienced at skipping we played 'lindes'; this was two longer ropes cawed simultaneously, while one or two people jumped trying to beat previous skipping records. I learned to play 'balls' firstly with one against the wall, and then with two singing songs such as 'E I Dominaca A I Chickaraka, Hum Bum Scoosh' and 'PK Penny Packet first you eat it then you crack it'. We birled, bounced and stotted the balls behind our backs and under our legs without dropping them. My brother and I excelled at marbles or dazzies and possessed the biggest and best 'tattie mashers' in Woodside, thanks to my dad and grandad who gave us all old ball bearings that were removed from the papermaking machines at Stoneywood Millls where they worked.

In the summer evenings families gathered outside, the women sitting on the window sills for a cleck, the men standing around smoking cigarettes and pipes, discussing the country's economy, football and politics as we got on with the evening play. Sometimes we put on a show that had been rehearsed during the day. Our epic was the Wizard of Oz, which ran for a week. The stage was set and cushions, blankets and chairs were placed out in the backie for our audience of friends, parents and neighbours. The boys would wear an old pair of men's trousers held up with braces, sporting moustaches and side burns carefully drawn on with eyebrow pencil. The girls would dress up in their mother's high heels, dresses trailing along the ground, wearing the brightest of red lipstick, the customary beauty spot and nail varnish. Heavily adorned with an assortment of glass beads and necklaces we would pretend to be the next Doris Day or Debbie Reynolds. We entertained in the Music Hall

Woodside, a place with a strong sense of its own community from the earliest days. (Aberdeen Central Library)

Our concert stage.

style learned from weekly visits to the Tivoli, the boys copying comedians like Jimmy Logan and Johnnie Beattie, the girls dancing and singing the latest songs of Alma Cogan and Ruby Murray.

Dressing up and acting were a big part in our playing time, pretend families with mum, dad, children with hoosies and shoppies all set up in the greenie. Docken seeds for mince and mud pies in the butcher shop, along with various grasses and shrubs for the greengrocers. We occasionally had seasonal berrics, rhubarb and carrots in our shoppie, chored (stolen) from the neighbouring allotments every year! Part of the back green was called a bleaching green and we were not allowed to play there as newly washed white cottons and linens were laid on the grass to bleach in the sun. We had to obtain permission to play in the back greenie, and if it was my granny's day for the wash house, we would help fill the huge boiler with water. Once it was stoked and fired, she would spend most of the day there boiling sheets, underwear, table linen, scrubbing clothes and if there was hot

The scene of many adventures, with air-raid shelter on the right.

Woodside school.

water left all the kids were popped in the tub to be bathed, girls first and then the boys.

One summer we formed a gang and had to take an oath of friendship never to be broken, followed by a dare that demanded we had to jump seven foot off the air-raid shelter. After plucking up courage I jumped and my knees hit my chin and my teeth went through my lip. Once over the trauma, I was shown the proper way to land and completed my jump successfully and was then deemed brave enough to be a member of the gang. My initiation ceremony was finally completed by having to drink from the cup of friendship. This was an old cracked cup with no handle containing the potion made from a mixture of toothpaste, baking soda, vanilla essence, milk and any other ingredient that was pinched from our mothers' pantries.

A beach picnic would be organised during the summer school holidays and fifteen to twenty children and adults would set off early the following morning to walk to the beach. Armed with picnic boxes, rugs, towels, buckets and spades, we would be on our way to claim a pitch as near to the main beach area as possible. We were in and out of the water all day, making sandcastles, burying each other up to our necks in sand. We wore plastic sandals and little rubber pumps and a variety of costumes made from cotton all bubbled up by shirring elastic or hand-knitted costumes and swimming trunks which stretched out of all proportion. The women wore boned costumes with billowing skirts and sparkly plastic-rimmed sunglasses. There would be music playing through loud speakers, donkey rides, beauty contests and sandcastle compet-

Woodside Parish church.

itions. On leaving the beach late in the afternoon we would line up for a 'cappie' – a huge ice cream cone drizzled with strawberry sauce; or a stick covered in candy floss.

We looked forward to returning to school at the end of August as the first Thursday back was Timmer Market. We were taken, as a treat that evening, to be bought a toy. These were mainly handmade from wood (timmer), whistles, monkeys on a stick, balsa planes and birds tied to a stick that whistled when you whirled them. The boys favoured the pea-pluffers as they blew dried pulses mercilessly at each other, and chased the girls round the playground the next day. A lot of our toys were home made, which included empty syrup cans that had holes bored for twine to be threaded through to hold on to as we clanged about. As we grew older we graduated to stilts made from two long pieces

of wood with footrests nailed on about two feet up the wood. After hours of practice we gained the skills to keep us vertical. Then came my brother's much-loved cairtie made from spare wood, and long awaited wheels from a neighbour's old pram. We would hurl the cairtie everywhere and added a bike horn, an old bit of carpet and a feather cushion for comfort. The brakes often failed and we had to use our feet to stop us crashing as we raced other cairties on the hillocks beside the Fountain. The cairtie had practical uses, often helping elderly neighbours struggling with heavy shopping. We also carried coal from my granda's coal store to people whose coal delivery was late.

During the autumn school holidays the cairtie proved its usefulness when collecting for the annual Guy Fawkes bonfire celebrations. Every street had a bonfire piled high with wood, newspapers, old linoleum and anything that would burn. Adults and children looked forward to the night with equal excitement, everyone had a role to play. Rivalry from the other streets existed and often at night older lads would raid other bonfires, inevitably leading to counter raids. The night before, the precious pyres would be guarded past bedtimes. Our mums made our guy; he was dressed in old clothes and stuffed with hay and old newspapers. We traipsed him round the nearby streets on the cairtie, knocking on neighbours' doors asking for 'a penny for the guy?' With our pennies we were allowed to buy fireworks and sparklers. Our dads lit the bonfire and made sure we were all safe before letting off the fireworks, then set light to our precious sparklers so we could draw our names in the night air before they fizzled out. We roasted potatoes and ate them as we watched the bonfire start to die down. Only then did we reluctantly head for home, the smell of smoke in our hair, gloves and coats and that wonderful feeling that still fills your heart with joy at the memory of another wonderful bonfire night.

Winter evenings were times when, once we had eaten our tea, completed our chores and finished our homework, we were encouraged to read, play cards and board games with all our family. The evening ended in our pyjamas, hugging a huge tin mug filled with cocoa and a thick slice of bread toasted with a fork at the fire, smothered in home-made jam. Then it was off to bed with a favourite book, often The Famous Five or the *Bunty* and *Hotspur* comics, as our parents and grandparents listened to their favourite radio programmes.

Other winter activities included attending the Brownies and the Lifeboys at Woodside Parish church, which was Church of Scotland, and going to Sunday school. Each Sunday a paragraph of text had to be learned by heart and recited out loud. I was awarded a prize for excellence in text repetition, a book called

Shirley & Co, which I still have with bits chiselled off the cover by my pet budgie. The word would go out at school that the Salvation Army were showing cartoon films in their hall. Just about every kid in Woodside would turn up, we would sing happy hymns and say a prayer before the roar would go up as the films started. In Woodside all church doors were open to the children , regardless of denomination, as were the hearts of our neighbours in Don Street, making it the happiest of places to belong.

Jacqueline Beattie

A family in Old Aberdeen

They smile at us from some long-gone, golden afternoon. A moment in time preserved by the Box Brownie. But how can we know what their time was really like? If we have listened carefully to the family stories, then we will have something other than a frozen second of the past. We will have some notion of the vibrant, living time that it was. For true history lies in anecdote, and largely in the anecdote of the ordinary man and woman. The really important things are, arguably, not the great events. Thornton Wilder, the American dramatist, wrote of how a thousand years from now people should know, 'This is the way we were: in our growing up and in our marrying and in our living and in our dying'. If we are at all interested in where we ourselves came from, can we disagree?

Old Aberdeen, where my family lived for generations, is now something of a quiet and almost quaint backwater, picturesque, enthused about in tourist guides and watched over by a local Heritage Society. It is largely a university campus, busy only in term time, but it was not always so. Even in my boyhood in the fifties it still retained the character of a busy, working, mixed community; an example of town and gown rubbing along amicably.

Generations.

But let's go further back to that window into a distant past which our photograph affords us. Let's listen to the whispers and the echoes of their stories as I attempt to recall them bringing that past to moving, colourful life.

The dawning of the last century ushered in the golden Edwardian afternoon, that final time of innocence and peace before the Great War changed lives for ever, and brutally forced the world into the modern age. Old Aberdeen basked in that sunshine. True, its glorious past as the community serving the great Cathedral of St Machar was long gone. Mitred and purple clad bishops no longer processed the cassies, of the Chanonry, nor did the wynds witness the passage of sober black-clad canons. The once powerful cathedral was simply a parish kirk, but the Aulton bustled now with housewives, servants, tradesmen and university types.

Amid this stir a young girl, my mother, played about the lanes in high summer. There was much to occupy a youngster in that place at that time; games around the 'needle's ee', the dark, narrow passageway at the back of the Townhouse, or a wander up the country track with the seemingly incongruous name 'Boathouse Brae' to see the trains clank and puff their way to Inverurie. But then, before the railway, it had been a canal and there had indeed been a boathouse at the top of what is now St Machar's Drive. If a daring mood took her and her younger sister, they might climb over the wall into the extensive gardens of Burnett of Powis, a local landowner whose grand house stood at the end of a long drive with the exotically twin-turreted gateway on the High Street. At times she would be called from her play to take the washing to 'Mangle Jean', an old woman who lived in Cat Mary's Lane and who wrung out clothes for a penny. In the stir of the High Street she would marvel at the professors' wives as they made their stately way to one of the many shops there. Fashion dictated long, sweeping elegant dresses and riotous ostrich feathered confections of hats, and a trip to the local shop was an event in those unhurried times.

Her family were not alien to fashion themselves, for her father was a respected independent tradesman, a slater who plied his trade around the Aulton. Indeed, he was something of a figure in the community as he had served a term as Master of the Local Lodge which met in the upper floor of the Townhouse. Two generations later I came across his sashes and regalia carefully wrapped in tissue paper and folded away in a long unopened drawer.

The family lived in one of the oldest houses in the High Street, set gable end to the street, as was the style of the older houses, and entered from Brewery Lane. As with many of the lanes running off the High Street, the name reflected something of the occupations of the inhabitants of the Aulton. There had been a brewery at one time and the house the family occupied had once been the home of the brewery manager, with the building at the end of the lane the stables and storage for the horse drawn drays. The only remnant of the Aulton Brewery now is the large decorated mirror advertising its beer which still hangs in the St Machar Bar at the top of the High Street. Another measure of the house's importance was the fire insurance medallion fixed to the outside, although for some reason it was removed and attached to a house further down the street where it remains still. It was a wonderful old house of hidden nooks and crannies, a twisting stairway, windows where windows shouldn't be and, its minor glory, a magnificent wood-panelled room overlooking the buzz of the High Street.

There were high days and holidays. The most notable was the annual St Luke's Fair, an event of great antiquity instituted in the same royal charter by which James IV granted 'Auld Aberdeen' the status of a burgh some four hundred years before. It was held in the glebe

The High Street, Old Aberdeen.
(Aberdeen Central Library)

adults who had been at work all day arrived to have their fun with much drinking and, no doubt, amorous fumblings in the garish light of the flickering flares.

An idyllic childhood, and indeed a time of peace and contentment for this tight little community which had only lost its separate burgh status a few years previously, at the end of the nineteenth century, and thus still retained a sense of its own identity. Life went busily on with little in the way of high drama.

And so it was with my forebears, although there was the odd incident of the telegram which arrived one sunny May morning. My grandfather opened it, read it with a grim face and locked it away, refusing to satisfy the natural inquisitiveness of the females of the house. Years later it came out that the news was of the hanging, out in the Wild West, of a relative, although the details never became clear. There was another relative, a dark, mumbling man living in a row of mean little cottages on the banks of the Don, who muttered of hiding a hoard of gold sovereigns in the bank of the river. He died poor, still muttering of his hidden treasure. (As a boy I went looking for it, but I never found anything...).

In far away Europe, however, the war clouds had been gathering and the storm burst upon the world and changed things forever. Even the Aulton could not remain immune, and my grandfather, the slater, put away his handbarrow, locked his shed and went off to war. In a sense he entered the modern world in more ways than one, for he was sent to the newly formed Royal Flying Corps to serve as ground crew on the new flying machines. There must have been something in the family genes which predisposed us to technological innovation because there is a newspaper cutting from the twenties which tells of a family member who built his own aeroplane, a thing apparently

field to the west of the High Street. Grandmother would dress my mother and her younger sister in their best and set off through Douglas Lane to enjoy the day. As evening drew on, however, the girls would be taken home again, for the fair was no place then for well-brought up young ladies. It became increasingly wild as the young not that uncommon in those pioneering days.

When the First World War was over, my mother ventured out of the confines of the old town into the wider world to find herself a job and a husband. The former she found in Lows, the bookseller which was situated in the airy loftiness of Aberdeen's New Market, that marvellous Victorian arcade which, crazily, was demolished in the 1960s, and the latter in the form of a young marine engineer. They set up home in Old Aberdeen and although her husband was an incomer from the City of Aberdeen, he was eventually accepted after a number of years. He was never, of course, ever regarded as an 'Aul Tooner', because, after all, his granny wasn't buried in the kirkyard at St Machar's.

He went off to sea and from time to time would blow in to the Aulton with tales from his travels around the globe. Thus the family and, on occasion, habitués of the gloomy, sawdust strewn St Machar's Bar, would hear of such far-away marvels as the Cape of Good Hope and Capetown, Sydney Harbour Bridge, the bustle of Calcutta, and so on. He was pretty good at telling them to me in later years and firing my imagination, so that after hearing them, you almost expected to step out of the front door and find yourself, not in the High Street, but on a dusty, sun-baked quayside in Mauritius, or at the foot of Table Mountain in Capetown. Or he would tell of a funeral at sea in the Indian Ocean; the perils of replacing steerage chains in the bowels of a ship in the middle of a night-time gale in the Bay of Biscay. He was an eyewitness to the politics of a changing world when he spoke of docking in Hamburg and seeing the growing problems in 1930s Germany, or an insight into European Empire with stories of natives being lashed by dockside overseers as they loaded cargo in Portuguese East Africa.

The war, which my father had seen the ominous signs of in his travels, broke out and again it lapped at the peaceful environs of the

Aulton. In the neighbouring yard a concrete air-raid shelter mushroomed, in the sylvan peace of Seaton Park a blockhouse was built among the trees, just below the towering spires of St Machar's, and an air-raid siren appeared on the Crown Tower of King's College. A grey and ominous time.

That Aberdeen was one of the most bombed cities in Britain after the major conurbations is well enough documented elsewhere, but how did it affect daily life for the inhabitants of this little corner, far removed from the great events playing out across the globe? The stories tell of a time which could be by turns desperate, fearful, bizarre and humorous. A neighbour hammers on the door to ask if she can hide her husband there as the police have arrived for him because he has refused the call-up. My mother, pregnant with me, scrambles beneath a coal lorry in Bedford Road as German

All dressed up for the fair.

College Bounds ,Old Aberdeen. (Aberdeen Central Library)

bombers fly overhead – there was talk of machine-gun bullets bouncing off the pavement in front of her, but that may be an exaggeration. My father, an ARP warden, spends nights discussing philosophy with one of the professors from the university as they stand on bomb watch at the top of the Cromwell tower in the university grounds My grandmother is sent out to investigate a metallic clang during an air raid, presumably as she is the oldest. It turns out to be a piece of corrugated iron, not an unexploded bomb or incendiary. A policeman from Woodside arrives to tell my grandmother that her inefficient blackout can be seen from two miles away in an otherwise darkened city.

Then it was all over and the Aulton, along with the rest of Britain, entered the era of post-war austerity. Changed days indeed from the golden dawning of the century forty-five years earlier. Indeed, Old Aberdeen had changed its character, as was inevitable. The old sense of a separate identity had almost gone, and the community looked more to the wider world of the City of Aberdeen for its daily needs. In truth, it was now physically a part of the burgeoning city whose buildings now touched and almost encircled the Aulton.

This is where I come into the picture and the memories become mine. I'll leave off now as my original theme was to show how the anecdotes of our predecessors can bring movement and colour to a vanished age and breathe life into the dry bones of historical fact, but we've got to learn to listen carefully while the storytellers are still with us.

Innes Murchie

The lion and the dogs

My granny lived in Ord Street, which, at the time I'm recalling, consisted of one large block of three tenements, each holding six houses, or rather flats as we would say nowadays. The photograph, taken from King's Gate by my father in 1922, might suggest that it was a prison or some other house of correction, standing on its own with only fields around it, but nothing could have been farther from the truth.

Rubislaw Quarry let the property to its employees, and a fine spirit of neighbourliness existed between all the tenants. Everybody knew everything about everybody else. They helped each other when help was needed; they sympathised, and meant it, when illness or death struck. They borrowed from each other, anything from a needle to an anchor-well, perhaps never an anchor but certainly a needle. I remember being in Granny's house, along with several other visitors, one New Year's Day when one of the little girls from upstairs came in. Looking wide-eyed round the fairly large assembly, she finally said, 'Mrs Paul, Ma's askin', can ye gi'e her the len' o' a needle an' threid to shoo up the hen's erse.'

Expressions ranged from shock to mirth to outrage, but Granny was unfazed. (I never knew her anything else). 'Surely, m'dearie,' she smiled, adding, when she handed over the darning needle and the reel of button thread, 'Tell yer Ma I hope ye a' enjoy yer New Year's denner.'

Most of the borrowed items were returned when the man of the house got his wages, for they were like one big family in a way, although no one intruded on anyone's privacy if it was obvious that intrusion was not welcome.

To come to the point of this story, Granny took in lodgers to make ends meet, and around 1932, when I was about ten or so, two of them kindly took me to the first house of the Tivoli to see a menagerie. Not to the stalls, the dress circle or even the upper circle, but right up to the balcony – the Gods! What a thrill!

It meant climbing what seemed like dozens of flights of stairs, and then, when we reached the top, picking our way carefully down the near-vertical steps to our seats. I can remember thinking that if I slipped and fell, I would be catapulted over the handrail at the bottom and land in the orchestra stalls, miles below. I could picture the toffs sat there watching as my lifeless body was scraped off

the floor, their nostrils flaring in disgust at the bloody mess that was left. I always had a fertile imagination.

I can't recall much about the actual show, although there would have been monkeys and all sorts of wild animals doing all sorts of tricks, but what stands out in my mind was the appearance of the lion. This act must have come immediately after the interval, because it would have taken a considerable time and effort to erect the vast barred enclosure on the stage. There was a sort of low tunnel at one side through which the animal would make his way into the cage itself. Excitement was building up, heightened by insistent rolls on the drums from the pit, until every member of the audience was sitting on the edge of his or her seat, eyes popping and breaths held in anticipation of the big moment.

The magnificent animal came through the entrance, slowly and majestically, as if giving people time to admire him, but at the last moment, when we waited anxiously for the tamer to crack his whip to show who was master, it gradually became evident that the lion was no longer behind bars. He was actually stalking along the front of the stage, just behind the footlights, looking for some way to jump off.

Pandemonium! Several screams accompanied the mass exodus of panic-stricken people, including the poor orchestra, as they fled from their seats and jammed the exits. We three, knowing that no lion could possibly scale all those stairs to reach *us*, sucked the Soor Plooms one of my escorts had bought earlier and watched the kerfuffle beneath us – on every level except ours. Even the lowering of the Safety Curtain didn't stop it.

The show was held up for not much more than thirty minutes, if I remember correctly. The lion had never got off the stage, and some of the menagerie hands had secured the broken link between tunnel and cage – the point where he slipped out – while others

Ord Street.

lured him back to where he should be. The errant audience filed back, in a more orderly fashion than they had gone out, and we finally got to see what we had come to see: The Lion Act. It was worth waiting for, the beast's growling and snarling making the act all the more suspenseful. I'm almost sure, though, that the tamer never put his head in the lion's mouth – I would have remembered if he had!

I must admit to being rather disappointed that the drama had ended so tamely and that nobody had been eaten alive, but it was still something to speak about. Even in those days, I could 'spikk the hin' legs aff a cuddly,' as Granny told me many times, so my friends had been tired of hearing about it... and perhaps a little jealous?

Another pre-war experience comes vividly back to me, but I had better set the scene to explain why I was where I was. I left school in June 1937 and found employment in the office of a wholesale confectioner. It was a small office, just one desk under the window, taking up the whole width of the room, with a shallow drawer at each side for our notebooks, pens, rulers, ink eradicator etc.,

and a deep drawer at each side to hold the day books and the ledgers we worked on.

Apart from myself, the office staff consisted of one lady of uncertain age – let's call her Helen. Tea breaks were unheard of then, but we bought soft drinks from the nearby soda fountain and stashed the bottles in the deep drawers behind the ledgers. We could only have wee 'scoffs' when the boss was out, but we were never at the stage where our tongues were hanging out with thirst. Hunger was staved off by helping ourselves to a 'few' sweets from the boxes on the table at our backs – samples of new lines, meant for customers to try before ordering for their shops, but our need was greater than theirs.

By the way, Malteser's were introduced somewhere between 1937 and 1938, and the office and warehouse staff had – dare I say it? – the lion's share. This could explain my ever-present craving for chocolate, now that I come to think about it. Helen, who became a great friend, also worked at the dog track on Saturday afternoons, and when she told me that I could have a job there if I wanted it, four shillings and sixpence per week –

the equivalent of 37.5 pence in today's money – so four shillings for two hours work was wealth indeed.

I can't recall exactly when I started working at the Dogs. I only remember the excitement surging up in me that first day when I came off the tramcar at the Bridge of Dee and walked to where Asda's store is now. Helen, who had obviously worked there for some time, showed me to where I'd be paying out to those who had backed the winners on the tote. It was an easy job, although I later had scabies on my hands from handling the money. (In case you wonder how I got rid of that, I had to use sulphur ointment and coal tar soap, *and iron my vest every day before putting it on*. Happy days?)

I was one of perhaps ten girls at a counter ten or twelve feet long, separated from the public by sliding hatches and fixed grilles, and I soon discovered an added bonus. We got tips! In some weeks, I collected much more than the 4/- I was paid.

Oddly, the best tips came from the small punters. For instance, someone picking up 7/6 might give me the sixpence, or a man getting 22/6 could give me the half crown. The serious gamblers on the other hand, those who placed large bets and whose winnings ran into hundreds of pounds, seldom left anything. I came to understand, of course, that they were part of a syndicate, each member having to get a share, so there was nothing to spare for tips.

What I'm about to describe happened on the last Saturday of the Glasgow Fair, so it was definitely July, and the year must have been 1938. It was a scorching hot day, and excitement was running high among the race-goers for some reason.

We were not supposed to watch what was going on outside our booth, but having finished paying out on one particular race, we took less time than usual to make ready for the next. Coins were in piles in front of us, well back from the grille – threepenny pieces, sixpences, shillings, florins and half crowns – and the notes in their cubby-holes – ten shillings, pounds, fivers and tenners. Pleased with ourselves, some of us slid open our hatches to see what we could see.

Guild Street, with the Tivoli on the left. (Aberdeen Central Library)

To be honest, we didn't see very much, there were too many people in the way, but we did catch sight of the electric bunny whizzing round with the greyhounds in hot pursuit. The noise level from supporters was deafening, and one Glaswegian got so carried away that he flung his jacket on to the track in front of the leader. The poor hound stopped, obviously wondering what he was supposed to do, and all the others halted behind him. All, that is, except the one who had been taking up the rear. He sauntered past as if he hadn't a care in the world…and came first!

A stunned silence fell, but when it was announced over the tannoy that payment would be made on this dog, there was an absolute riot.

'It's no' fair! Ma dog wiz winnin'!'

'Awa' an' bile yer heid! Bonnie Blue wid've won, the wye he was gaun.'

'Naw he widnae! He wiz tirin'. Joey's Boy wid've beat 'im.'

An Aberdonian put his tuppenceworth here. 'Hey min, fair's fair! Fa could ken fitt'n dog wid've won? An' that ane wiz first hame.' He was shouted down, and then another Glasgow voice made itself heard above the clamour. 'See youz lot? Youz jist open yer mooths an' let yer bellies rummel. Stop gaun oan aboot whit dog would've won, the race should be declared void. '

Dozens voiced their agreement to this. 'He's right! They cannae dae this! The race'll ha'e to be run again.'

The chorus swelled. 'Aye, run it again.'

But the management stood firm, and we paid only those who had backed the dog which, but for the action of one misguided man, should have come last. The crowd was in full war cry now, baying like a pack of hungry wolves, issuing threats to all and sundry. We shut the hatches in some relief as soon as the few sheepish winners had been paid and were fighting their way to the gate, but our troubles were not yet over.

A furious mob had gathered at every exit, waiting to confront any employee who had ventured out. No one did. It was an impasse, neither side giving way, and we girls hadn't helped by wailing that we wanted to go home. It was well over an hour later before someone thought of a way to help us. I've the feeling that a camp bed was used, but it could have been something more substantial. Whatever it was, we were able to stand on it to climb out through a window on the other side of the building.

I've no idea what happened after that – being the youngest, I was first to go, and tore off at the double, shooting up Holburn Street without looking back. When I asked Helen on Monday morning, she couldn't, or wouldn't tell me anything. All she said was

'The rules say the first dog past the post is the winner, no matter what'.

I don't know if either of these incidents ever hit the newspapers, but I've often wondered if anyone else can remember being at the Tivoli on the night the lion made a bid for freedom, or being at the dogs on that hot Saturday afternoon in July 1938. Not that it matters. It's water under the bridge, isn't it? An awful lot of water – the Tivoli episode was seventy years ago!

Incidentally, the block of tenements my granny lived in is still there but no longer stands on its own. If you should be cruising along King's Gate in a car at any time, and happen to look down Ord Street as you pass, you might just catch a glimpse of it amongst the bungalows and villas that have sprung up around it since the war. Once a far-flung outpost of the city, standing out starkly against the sky, the tenement building is today well within Aberdeen's western boundary, part of an upmarket area with a desirable address and postcode.

What would my granny have thought of that?

Doris Davidson

2 An Aberdeen Miscellany

Arms, oddities and errors: the story of Aberdeen's coat-of-arms

The ancient practice of heraldry marks, informs, decorates and identifies. The heraldry of Aberdeen is among the most widely used of any council in Scotland. Our town coat-of-arms appears on buildings, vehicles, road signs, furniture, clothing, books, badges, banners, bollards, furnishings, theatre tickets, even litter bins. Only Glasgow comes anywhere near matching our usage. Yet the origin of Aberdeen's symbolism is shrouded in mystery.

We know that our armorial ensigns are borne by authority of the patent granted in 1674 by Sir Charles Erskine, Lord Lyon King of arms. Lyon Erskine calls the Aberdeen arms as being 'of old, pertaining to the Royal Burgh of Aberdeen', thus confirming that the town heraldry was used here long before 1674.

What we now call heraldry first appeared on seals, the wax impressions which a millennium ago formed simple signature and identity. In Royal burghs such as Aberdeen, Banff and Montrose, the earliest seals generally showed the local saint. The first known use of a burgh seal in Aberdeen was in 1271 on a charter by Adam Gley in favour of the Black Friars, depicting St Nicholas. There is also a description of a burgh seal of around 1350, on the reverse of which is a building with a central doorway and three pyramidical spires each bearing a cross at the apex.

What these three spires or towers symbolise is open to question: Aberdeen Castle, the Mither Kirk of St Nicholas, or the Holy Trinity? This design reappears on the burgh seal used until 1424, a town wall of dressed masonry with a closed two-leaf gate in the centre and three spires or towers rising above the coping of the wall. While the immediate inference is that this is the burgh wall and the kirk of St Nicholas, it is more than coincidental that the representation of a three-towered gateway occurs in cities across Europe from Poland to Portugal, from Cracow to Oporto. Even more coincidental is that our nearest medieval trading partners of Bergen, Hamburg and Antwerp – all members of the Hanseatic League - not only bear arms similar to this seal, but also use red and silver as their city colours.

A major change comes in 1430, when a very different burgh seal shows a shield with a single tower enclosed by the familiar border or *tressure* of the royal arms of Scotland, and the shield supported by two lion-like animals holding between them a scroll on which are the words *Bon Accord*. The building is a triumphal arch rather than a tower and looks more European than our present three towers.

Why and when Aberdeen broke away from the European style of a three-towered gateway to today's version of three separate towers is a matter of speculation. The shield we recognise today appears alongside the name 'New Aberdeen' on the heraldic ceiling of 1520 in St Machar's Cathedral. A seal of 1537 repeats this; indeed there is some evidence for a

Seal of 1430.

similar seal to have been used as early as 1444. Aberdeen Castle had vanished by the reign of King Robert III (1390-1406), so why three towers? Do they remember the three fortifications of the Castle Hill, the Port Hill and St Catherine's Hill? There are plenty of stories, but few facts.

Similarly the matter of the border containing the towers: this Royal 'tressure' signifies great honour in heraldry. It would have been granted only by Royal command, and Perth is the only other burgh to have it. Tradition holds the name of King Robert Bruce as the donor, given for the help he received from the citizens in the War of Independence. This Bruce legend confuses both King David Bruce and his father King Robert. Equally King Robert is held to have granted the additional heraldic honour of leopard supporters and even to have been the source of the motto *Bon Accord,* reputedly the password used by townspeople in 1308 when they destroyed the castle of Aberdeen then held by the English. However, there is no evidence for any of this.

The erroneous story of our motto seems to have started with the heraldist Sir George Mackenzie of Rosehaugh, who in 1680 wrote:

'The Word *Bon-Accord* was given them by King Robert Bruce for killing all the English in one night in their Town, their Word being that night *Bon-Accord*'.

John Cruickshank, writing in *The Armorial Ensigns of the Royal Burgh of Aberdeen* (1888) states

'…the [present] armorial ensigns were substituted for the representations on the older seal [of 1430], *unquestionably* by grant of King James I'.

But no substantiation is offered as to why King James I (1406-37) should have made the grant. The necessary evidence may lie in missing council records. Our town records start in 1398, a matter of civic pride that such early records are almost complete to the present day. Unfortunately the only volumes missing cover the period 1414 to 1433, precisely when King James might have granted the arms. A Royal conferral would surely have been minuted. Unless and until these lost records are found, to precisely date the granting of arms to Aberdeen remains beyond us.

Nevertheless there is a strong tradition that suggests James granted both the arms and the tressure and supporters. While legend does not compete in accuracy with historical fact, the firmness of belief in the corpus of Aberdeen thinking that the arms stem from King Jamie suggest that – as with the tale of King Robert Bruce and the spider – it may be that folk memory carries the day. Certainly James held Aberdeen in enormous gratitude for the assistance the burgh gave in underwriting his Royal expenses during exile in England.

The leopard supporters have a rare existence in Scots heraldry, with only

Aberdeen using these beasties, but as ever with our town heraldry, nothing is straightforward, for the familiar leopard supporters actually originated as lions, as the seal of 1430 clearly shows; doubters only have to look at their manes. The transformation from lions to leopards arises from confusion over early French terminology. The heraldic language of *blazon* is French based. The French lion is our lion rampant; our lion passant is their *leopard-lionne*, while our lion rampant guardant is their *lion-leoparde*. In early heraldry, any lion that was not rampant was termed a *lion leoparde*. 'Leopard' was later applied to a lion *passant guardant*, a lion standing on three paws, right paw raised, face outwards and tail curled over its back. Three of these lions form the royal arms of England, hence the expression 'the leopards of England'.

The Letters Patent matriculating the arms of 1674 mention the shield as being 'supported by two leopards *Proper* (in their natural colours)', meaning that each faced the shield. Unfortunately, the herald painter who created the accompanying picture showed the supporter on the right with face in profile, but the left as full-faced. In spite of a directive by Lord Lyon George Burnett in 1883 clearly stating that both leopards should be in profile, there remains confusion throughout the city to this day, as witnessed by the different attitudes adopted by supporters on the burgh arms show on the Mercat Cross, on Aberdeen Grammar school and in the many examples in wood, stone and glass in the Town House and on the staircase of the Town and County Hall. The splendid granite carving above the balcony on the Town House shows the leopards correctly facing each other, but interestingly the muscular beasts depicted are lions rather than leopards.

Lord Lyon Sir Charles Erskine's re-grant of burgh arms in 1674 followed a disastrous fire in Edinburgh in 1670 when Scottish heraldic records were lost. As a result, an Act of the Scots Parliament in 1672 charged all who had

Seal of Aberdeen until 1424.

previously borne arms to re-matriculate, giving us the arms in use to this day: *Gules, three towers triple towered within a Royal tressure Argent,* supported by *two leopards Proper,* and the motto *Bon Accord*.

Silver towers on a red shield explain why the city livery colours are red and white, and why Aberdeen Football Club plays in the same colours. Curiously, Aberdeen is alone among Scotland's cities in not having a crest above the arms.

Good examples of city heraldry can be found on the Mercat Cross in the Castlegate, along with granite carvings on the Grammar school, the 'Monkey House' (the CGNU building), the War Memorial and the Town House. There are also painted stone panels on Marischal College and the Elphinstone Building, plus many fine examples in wood, stone and glass inside the Town House.

As ever, Aberdeen bears a final sting in the heraldic tail. It is one of only four burghs with two coats-of-arms, the others being Kirkcaldy, Linlithgow and Montrose. These alternative *sacred bearings* show St Nicholas, patron saint of Aberdeen, dressed as a bishop above three children in a cooking pot. The original

These ensigns of Aberdeen appeared first in 1883.

Early eighteenth-century representation of the Burgh Arms.

Nicholas rescued three children who, during a great famine, were salted in a tub prior to being cooked. St Nicholas is the patron saint of children, sailors and pawnbrokers, as well as being the original Santa Claus.

Gordon Casely

A history of The Green

Far's there an aul road in Aiberdeen?
The Green
Far'd sooth intrince ti the toon hae been?
The Green
Doon Hardgate and the Windmill Brae,
Beggars, nobles, aa come they,
Across the Bow Brig n throo which way?
The Green

Fit road in toon wis the King's Highway?
The Green
Far's there a pub named that the day?
The Green
There wis Royals in coach n armies on foot,
Some passin throo n some takin root,
Fit Wye did they tak ti the toon nae doot?
The Green

Far wis the hoos eh Bruce n Queen?
The Green
Far hid a market ayewis been?
The Green
Far fisher wives selt fish n dukes,
Crabs n kippers they selt tulls,
Far cood ye feel the toon's hairt pulse?
The Green

Far'd Toon Baillies civil war declare?
The Green
N commit a bloody offence where?
The Green
They shot Montrose's drummer, then,
Ee sacked the toon wi troops n men,
N far wis it thit he hid come in?
The Green

Fit wye hid Cumberland come throo toon?
The Green
Far wis ee's troops aa camped aroon?
The Green
For six weeks bade n caused disgrace,
Prince Charles n men wis fa ee chase,
N ee come throo, fit wis the place?
The Green

Throo far'd Robbie Burns come wi coach?
The Green
N fit did the Back Wynd use ti approach?
The Green
Fin it wis at the fit o a brae,
Nae cut aff n hiddin like the day,
Union Street it made fit that way?
The Green

Far wis loons teen fin they wir 'list'?
The Green
N far the hoose kept till mist?
The Green
Then smuggled oot and then awa,
On the tide ti America,
Fit wis it thit the loons last saw?
The Green

Fit hid the Denburn at it's west en?
The Green
N follyin that the Great North Train?
The Green
The aul Bow Brig wis teen awa,
Nae mair ti cairry coach or car,
Far wis an iron brig then saw
The Green

Far wis Littlejohn's grocery store?
The Green
Fit hid a teapot owre a shop door?
The Green
Far wis a 'Mannie' on a well,
N hooses doon throo chimneys fell?
N far did aa that happen, pray tell?
The Green

The Green is central to Aberdeen history. The Mannie's in the middle.(Aberdeen Central Library).

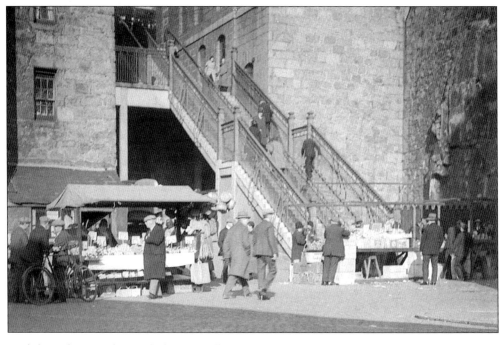

Far hid a market ayewis been? (Aberdeen Art Gallery and Museums Collection).

Far'd William the Lion's hoose nae face?
The Green
Far'd Carmelite Friars hae their base?
The Green
Far wid wi hae ti look the day
Ti get this history knowledge fae?
Believe me fin Eh say it's nae,
The Green

E. Davidson

A generous act of charity?

'Proctor's Kirkville Orphan Training Home' is situated on the western outskirts of Aberdeen city. Founded in 1892, it was one of the few establishments set up to address the problem of unwanted and orphaned children that managed to survive beyond its centenary.

The apparent generosity of James Proctor of Tarland is less clear cut when there is further examination of how he acquired his wealth. In 1854 his cousin, Margaret Gordon McPherson, at the age of nineteen, was the major beneficiary of the wealth accrued by her mother's unmarried brother. Alexander Grant had been living in Jamaica and profited well from the slave labour that was used on his plantations. Her parents received a £1,000 annuity in his will and so moved to Edinburgh, purchasing Lauriston Castle. Margaret adopted the Grant name, moved to the Aberlour Estate and became engaged in various philanthropic schemes, which were funded from part of the £300,000 inherited from her uncle. Her social status had been greatly elevated and she relied heavily on Mrs Gordon, her maternal widowed aunt, and Bishop Eden for friendship and advice. In 1864 she met an interesting woman at a weekend gathering of friends at her mansion. Margaret persuaded the woman, Miss Temple, to return the following year as her companion and she became an important part of Margaret's life.

The Scottish Episcopal Church had also become Margaret's religious support in her early twenties, via her contact with Bishop Eden. She was told about Reverend Jupp who was in poor health due to his zealous work in poor communities in the north-east of England. He accepted her generous offer to become her chaplain in 1874, with several provisos to allow him to continue his work to alleviate the suffering of the poorer classes, especially for children. Despite the area being strongly Scottish Presbyterian, Margaret agreed to fund the erection of a grand Episcopal church in Aberlour. In April 1874 she also financed the building and staffing of an orphanage school at Craigellachie, and a similar one was planned for Charleston of Aberlour.

Margaret's companion had formed a secret relationship with a male guest who was attending a social function at Aberlour. In January 1876 Miss Temple left Aberlour and married Captain Yeatman shortly afterwards. It was a very upsetting time for Margaret who became depressed and severely ill. She felt it was a betrayal of their special relationship, so Margaret decided to remove the now Mrs Yeatman from any entitlement to the Aberlour estate. It was done hastily using a local lawyer, and the full implications of this action became public when Margaret died suddenly on 14 April 1877, aged forty-three years.

It became known that in 1865, after Miss Temple moved to Aberlour, the two women had participated in a type of matrimonial ceremony. Miss Temple wore a ring provided by Margaret, and a new will had been drawn up making Miss Temple the major beneficiary to the Aberlour fortune which totalled £71,000 plus the estate. Now, not only had she revoked the inheritance to her former companion, she had also voided the rest of her will. There was a long debate about her intentions when the various claimants to her estate came to court to fight for their share of the fortune.

The relationship between the two women was examined with detailed evidence being given by the butler and maids. Issues surrounding a mysterious fire and an unexplained illness of Margaret's were also brought to the public's notice. In November 1877 the House of Lords was asked to determine whether Margaret had died intestate. Mrs Yeatman tried to prove that Margaret Gordon McPherson Grant was 'not of sound mind' when she revoked her will and therefore it was not legal. The Proctor family were the heirs-in-law, despite their being no contact with her paternal cousins and no mention of them in any of her wills. Margaret's dislike of these relatives was also reported in the local press coverage.

Mrs Yeatman accepted a £10,000 compromise settlement. The prearranged funding of the various local philanthropic projects was to end by December 1877. Reverend Jupp appealed against this, but in 1879 it was denied. This was a major catastrophe, especially for the four boys who had already been moved into Burnside Cottage on the Aberlour Estate.

The paternal cousins of Margaret inherited quite a fortune. James and Margaret lived locally, but some of it went abroad to America, Australia and New Zealand.

Until 1872 education had been mostly provided by the Church. The Government then decided it would be the responsibility of the State to provide basic education for all younger children. This compulsory education gave regular contact with children and so highlighted the lack of welfare provision. Each parish had to take care of its own poor and sick, and relied heavily on donations from benefactors and charitable groups. They employed 'Inspectors of Poor' to organize the distribution of aid from a central parish fund, to alleviate misery and suffering caused by abject poverty.

The founder of Proctors Home, James Proctor, was born in 1823 son of Alexander, a watchmaker from Tarland. He had six older brothers and a younger sister. He followed his father's profession, and in 1851 was living in the village with his parents and sister Margaret.

When he was thirty-eight years old James moved to Aboyne and rented 350 acres of farmland called Braeroddach. On 7 June 1866 he married Ann Hector of Udny, whose family had strong connections with the Church. Ann was three years younger than James so they would probably have little expectation of having their own children.

Margaret Proctor continued to live at Tarland, and had taken in a family to lodge with her. The head of the family, Mr Joseph Firth, was a watchmaker by trade and probably continued the Proctor business in the village. Mr Firth was also an Inspector of the Poor in Tarland. This contact would give James the opportunity to hear first hand accounts of the conditions of the destitute families in the parish, and could have influenced his decision, at a later date, to fund a 'Cottage Home'.

He had been farming at Aboyne but with his inheritance, bought and moved to the estate of Kirkville at Kirkton of Skene and took ownership of a second home, Tarland Villa at Ballater.

His sister Margaret used her share to move initially from Tarland to Carden House next to Aberdeen Grammar school, and then transferred to a house she had built in 1882 at 3 Queens Gate. It was called Badentoy after the estate at Banchory-Devenick, which she had purchased on 11 February 1881.

In 1879 James lodged the first of several letters with the Sheriff of Aberdeen bequeathing part of his wealth 'for a useful charitable purpose' after his death. This letter mainly involved the identification of the Trustees:

Provost of Aberdeen

Four Senior Magistrates

Two Resident Sheriffs

Proctor Kirkville's Orphan Training Home.

Procurator Fiscal of Aberdeen
Established Church minister of Skene
Free Church minister of Skene
Chairman of Skene school board
Established Church minister of parish of Tarland

Subsequent letters gave further detail of the aims and organization of the 'home'. He stipulated that the children should 'acquire skills' of agriculture and housekeeping. He gave an option on three sites within his estate for the erection of the home, with accompanying land for cultivation. On admission, he preferred the children to be 'from five to seven years' and that 'they should be retained from four to six years.' He limited the number in the home to ten, with two of these places being reserved for 'natives of

Tarland or Vale of Cromar'. It was to be called 'Proctor's Christian Industrial Cottage Home'.

On 14 February 1884 he wrote a letter referring to the mode of management, emphasising the Christian character as regards training, education and upbringing. The children were to be 'poor, destitute orphan children of parents of the industrial classes. Honest, moral and of irreproachable sober habits of good repute, unstamped by vice or crime, approved eligible and fit for the Home by the Trustees and managers appointed under the Trust'. The name was now to be changed to Proctors Kirkville Orphan Training Home. He mentioned Quarriers Home at Bridge of Weir Glasgow as an example of what he hoped to create.

The Bannermans were early house-parents.

Kirkton House., c. 1915.

Kirkton House today; little has changed.

James Proctor died on the 31 January 1888 and the first meeting of the appointed Trustees was on 23 April of that year. The site on Kirkton Farm was agreed upon. The post of house-parents was advertised in the Aberdeen Journal on 23 and 25 November 1892. There were eighty-one applications. Three orphans were accepted by the Trustees to be brought to the home as soon as it was ready. It was officially opened in 1893.

The housemother was to run the home, feeding and clothing the children and giving the girls experience of house-keeping, which included cooking, laundry, needlework, knitting, poultry and dairy. The housefather was to manage the land and animals and give the boys experience of agriculture, gardening and animal husbandry. The produce was to be used by the home and any excess to be sold on or swapped locally, to provide necessities for the home. Children could also help on neighbouring farms, especially during harvest time. The trustees would make a yearly inspection visit, sometimes marked with a token personal gift to the children.

By 15 December 1945 there were thirteen children in the Home, all from Aberdeen City Public Assistance Committee. In the 1950s the home started to use its capital to cover its running costs. It increased its boarding rate to '35/-'. In 1961 children were referred from the Children's Department of Aberdeen Town Council. The board and lodging rate was £2 2s per week. By the end of the sixties the Trustees noted that the Social Services were developing and felt that the home should 'be in more specialist hands'. They finally agreed in April 1969 that Aberdeen County Council could take over the factoring and also maintain the property. The fields adjoining the house were rented out to a local farmer and the animals gradually sold off. It was used as a family unit, providing long-term care. Sibling groups were referred by the Social Work Department for admittance to the home.

In 1975 responsibility was transferred to Grampian Regional Council due to reorganisation. It accepted children aged eight to sixteen, needing both long and short-term care. The social work policy had now changed to focus on giving children the opportunity to belong to a family of their own. They were encouraged to develop in ways that would allow them to return to their own families or move on to join a new family. The older adolescents were supported to acquire skills that would help them transfer to independent living, as it was unlikely that a substitute family would be available to older children. The maximum number of children had by this time been reduced to eight. This had come from a mixture of policies regarding children's rights, expectations and an acknowledgement of the emotional problems that were now evident in many of the children who were referred. The staffing ratio had also been increased to allow opportunity for more extended contact between children and adults. It was expected that the staff would be willing to undertake training, which would help them to deal with the daily problems that emerged from the individual and the cumulative effects of living in a group environment.

When there was further local government re-organisation in the 1990s it was again managed and funded by Aberdeenshire Social Work Department. The first royal visit occurred in August 1993 when Princess Anne was guided round the premises. The new housing estates around Westhill continue to expand westward towards the home, and it is gradually becoming less isolated within the community. Several homes in the area closed as social work policy continued to try to reduce the necessity for establishments to provide a home base for young people and client numbers diminished.

The Proctor family had denied Reverend Jupp the finances that he needed to fulfil his and Miss McPherson-Grant's dreams.

Clearing the land.

Experience in agriculture was a mainstay of the home's training program.

Proctor's in 1992.

Proctor's in 1992.

Centenary celebrations.

The driveway to a new future for many.

He persevered with their philanthropic goal and managed to locate another local benefactor to allow the Aberlour Orphanage to expand to its envisaged capacity of 500 children. Education and work experience were provided for everyone, with a view to creating model citizens for their expected role in life. Support was also offered for those who required help with the transition to adulthood and life beyond Aberlour. It was not so high profile as Barnardo's and Quarrier's, who started around the same time, as it did not expand beyond the locality. The Aberlour Child Care Trust still exists today, though with a higher profile and in a more modern format of small units within local communities throughout Scotland.

The Proctors Children's Home celebrated its Centenary in 1992 with the help of the local community of Westhill and Skene, who initiated 'Friends of Proctors.' There were many happy and emotional reunions that day. Jessie Kesson who lived there as a child from 1925-1932 was disappointed that she was unable to attend, but the Lord Provost of Aberdeen mentioned her in his speech, pointing out her successful writing career. Her early novel *The White Bird Passes* is autobiographical and includes memories of her time at Proctors. Her return visit to the home had been in October 1989 when she was seventy-three years old. The quieter setting at that time had allowed her space to contemplate and share her vivid memories without disturbance or distractions.

Jessie Kesson would probably have been able to use the history behind the funding of Proctor's Home to create a story filled with scandal, intrigue, romance and family feuds. The legacy in James Proctor's will was to create an orphanage which has perpetuated his name. We can debate whether this was a purely philanthropic act or initiated by a guilty conscience – but the truth will remain within the family.

Pamela Tate

Aberdeen's trams

For so many, private transport has become one of the ever-increasing necessities of modern life. Where would we be without a car?

It wasn't always like this, however, and in the city of Aberdeen, like all the others where traffic was much lighter in the years immediately after the Second World War, getting from A to B for a lot of us was a public matter. For the generation before the last one, as a matter of course, one took to the urban railroad that was the tram, known ironically enough as 'the car'.

In the mid-1950s, when I was a boy, the population of Aberdeen was just under the 200,000 mark, quite a leap from the corresponding figure of just over 80,000 in the 1870s. I mention the latter period, and 1874 in particular, because it was in that year that the first trams appeared in the Granite City – a mere half-dozen, pulled by horses, and overseen by the Aberdeen District Tramways Company. It is interesting to note that in this eighty-year period the suburbs of Aberdeen mushroomed by a factor of four, while the population of the city itself grew at just half that rate.

So from the turn of the century onwards it was becoming more and more commercially viable to provide the public transport system that the trams did. With a ticket costing anything from a halfpenny to two pence, it is no wonder the car became such a part of our local culture for over half of the twentieth century.

This became more recognisable from 1898 when the town council (The Corporation Tramways) took over its running, and laid on a wider range of routes – for example, out to Bieldside and Bankhead.

Now, more and more trams were being put into commission and then came the conversion to electric power. The system

Union Street in the 1920s. (Aberdeen Central Library)

became ever more successful because it was cheap to use, and frequent. At peak times, trams were leaving major pick-up points (for example St Nicholas Street) every two minutes! By the 1920s a staggering fifty million people rode the Aberdeen trams every year. A mere twenty years later, at the time of the Second World War, the corresponding annual figure was approaching seventy million, and this despite the abandonment of some of the more suburban routes in the late 1920s.

My single most enduring memory of the whole tram era as I experienced it (we are talking the 1950s here) is the image of the tram conductor hurriedly changing the seats over – from one direction to the other – at the tram terminus, at the very bottom of Holburn Street, where the big roundabout at the Bridge of Dee now stands. The journey had ended, perhaps from Union Street in the city

centre, or from even further afield, and his passengers were waiting to start their journey into town. In an era of greater social cohesion, the tram seemed to have become a theatre for the tapestry of life and, more often than not, the conductor was the star of the show.

Indeed, as a boy I had become convinced, as I still am, that the prime qualification for his job was a ready and unforced facility to address and absorb the concerns and troubles of humanity, while at the same time dispensing measured sympathy and appropriate humour. Well, that's how it seemed at any rate.

But in any case, alas, by the 1950s, to the wider world the trams had become no longer fashionable, and the council in its wisdom decided to abandon them. The very last Aberdeen tramcar ran in 1958, and now, over forty years later, the only survivor of Aberdeen's entire tram era is one of the first horse-drawn variety which led the Jubilee procession back in 1924. It is housed in Edinburgh's Transport Museum.

To Aberdonians of a certain age, the tram lines are becoming more and more of a distant memory: any physical remnant of the tram age removed when the lines were all finally lifted from the city and its environs.

Of course it was prevailing economic imperative that killed off trams – put to the torch at Aberdeen Beach like subversive witches on that May evening in 1958. To many, perhaps uninitiated in the wisdom of economics, or merely stubborn in their nostalgia, the occasion, not without its drama and symbolism, has always seemed more of an execution than a natural passing – a punishment for the crime of being out of date.

Yet, now all those years down the line (so to speak), as we sit cocooned in the daily traffic jams, within or approaching the city, there is a nagging sense that the dream of the motor car has now gone at least a little bit sour. As the amount of cars using our roads soars, we long for solutions to the problems of which we ourselves are the major part.

Over the last few decades, ironically in the time since the demise of the tram, other major cities, here and abroad, are turning once more to the advantages of urban rail transport in a bid to conquer their daily choking traffic jams. These attempts have gone from strength to strength.

Perhaps it makes sense, once again, to travel by tram.

Alan Morrice

By the fifties, buses were taking over.

Grave robbers and the St Fittick's church

As children, we played in the ruins of an old coaching inn which was reputed to be haunted. In daylight, along with other Torry children, we would play hide and seek around the old charred wooden stairs. There were no banisters and there were many gaps and cracks in the crumbling walls. The stairs led to an upper floor but there were no floorboards left, only a few blackened heavy beams. The more daring of the boys, despite the warnings to stay out of the ruins, would clamber about these beams with an apparent total disregard for their own safety. None were brave enough, however, to play in the ruins at night when many claimed that they could hear an eerie, wailing sound which was said to be coming from the 'haunted' building. Of course, many old buildings are claimed to be haunted, but perhaps the following account explains why this particular inn acquired its reputation.

The inn was situated a few hundred yards from the harbour in Old Torry. It was the last building in a row of two-roomed owner-occupied fisher folk's houses in Fore Close, a few hundred yards from the quayside. To its right-hand side, looking from the foot of the sloping close, were houses. Facing them on the left were the outside toilets and wash houses.

The tavern towered over the cottages, for it was the only building in Torry at that time with an upper floor which held the bedrooms. Downstairs was the public house where local villagers would join bonafide travellers for a glass of ale. Joined to the rear of the building was a small stable where horses were fed and watered.

Despite the Anatomy Act of 1832, body snatching was still prevalent. Professors in universities and teachers of anatomy would pay large sums of money in return for freshly buried corpses on which they would carry out their research on the human body. It was due to the nefarious schemes of one pair of resurrectionists, as they were called, that the Torry Tavern was razed to the ground.

Almost two miles away from the inn, on the road from Torry to Cove Bay, lay St Fittick's church, now unfortunately another ruin. The church stood on its own, a short distance from the rough dirt road. It was surrounded by a churchyard, part of which was assigned to the private use of Colonel Davidson, the Laird who owned most of the surrounding land and who lived in a large house on Balnagask Road. His allocation of burial ground was laid with cement paving stones, to prevent ravage from those evil men who desecrated graves for their greed of money.

Dark and late one night, two resurrectionists, bent on their villainous business, crept into the cold yard. With them they had to bring the equipment required for their macabre task. A wooden handcart was required to remove the body. Lying on this, covered by sacking, would be a shovel and ropes. Although the wooden wheels of the cart had no rubber tyres, they managed to be extremely quiet as they trundled it along the dirt road. Once inside the burial grounds, they soon found the fresh mound of earth denoting that morning's funeral. Whilst one man dug, the other kept watch and soon they uncovered the coffin. After manoeuvring it up to ground level, they quickly prised the lid off, removed the body and tossed it on to the handcart. The shovel and ropes quickly followed and all were covered by the sacking before the two men scampered.

As they neared the old tavern, having pushed the burden for nearly two miles, they must have decided that it was thirsty work, and entered the bar to quench their thirst. Before doing so, they pushed their macabre load into a corner of the empty stable and threw some straw form the stable floor over their cart. Once in the bar, one drink followed

My christening.

another until suddenly there was the sound of a whistle and two policemen entered the saloon. The two guilty men must have assumed that their crime had been discovered, and while the officers were questioning the bartender, they slipped out of the bar and hurried to the stable to decide what to do. They must have thought it too risky to take the cart out. Whether it was due to panic, induced by their drunken state, or by deliberate design to get rid of the evidence, they set fire to the straw in the stable and disappeared into the darkness.

The smell of smoke soon alerted the men in the saloon. Someone shouted fire, creating an instant panic as the customers all rushed to the doors, trying to escape into the courtyard. One policeman organised a bucket-chain while the other pedalled off on his bicycle to alert the fire brigade. All was in vain, however. The blaze spread to the tavern and by the time the horse-drawn fire brigade arrived the old inn was practically gutted. The nearest cottagers, rather than saving the inn, had naturally been more intent on soaking the exposed parts of their own houses and this limited the damage to them. The two strangers were blamed for starting the blaze but they had made good their escape and were never caught.

Next morning, when the partially cremated body was found, it was first assumed that it was the body of a tramp who had taken illegal shelter for the night. But when the truth emerged, as the empty coffin and open grave were discovered, pandemonium set in. The thought of resurrectionists in their midst struck terror in the hearts of the villagers. Talk of and comparison with those most infamous body snatchers, Burke and Hare, was rife. People still recalled the gruesome trial in 1828 of Burke and Hare and the resulting death by hanging of Burke in 1829.

Following the incident, parents kept a strict watch on their offspring and panic set in. 'We

My grandparent's gravestone.

could have all been murdered in our beds' was the prevailing cry, for it had been proved that, in the past, unscrupulous body snatchers would commit murder for the sole purpose of selling the dead bodies to the equally unscrupulous medical men. In fact, it was acknowledged at the trial of Burke and Hare that they had done so. The relatives of the resurrected man had, of course, to have him re-interred this time, they hoped, to rest in peace.

The old St Fittick's church has long since fallen into disrepair, although why this is so appears to be lost forever. I often wonder if the roof was demolished to save having to pay taxes. The first memory I have of it was when all the pews were gone, along with other church equipment, and the interior used as an extension of the burial ground.

I can also remember that, by the right-hand side of the church entrance, there lay the remains of implements of punishment. I found

OLD KIRK OF ST. FITTICK.

St Fittick's Kirk. (Aberdeen Art Gallery and Museums Collection)

out that one had been called a scold and this was used, as its name suggests, to clamp the mouth of a nagging wife.

Another implement was used to chain young maidens who had been foolish enough to fall into the 'family way', as the saying went. The unmarried pregnant girl would have to stand there in shame as the so-called Christian congregation filed past. The story goes that she would be spat on and verbally vilified by those worshippers! But what of the man who was responsible for her condition? No word of punishment for him. He could even have been one of those passing her by with scorn, averting his eyes as he entered the church.

Another memory was of a stone tablet, made of granite I think, which was fastened to the left-hand side of the outside wall at the gate. A chiselled inscription read that St Columba had visited St Fittick's and there he had sprinkled holy soil over the burial ground with the result that the graves would be free from worms. The stone tablet was still there when I was a teenager in the late 1920s and I would love to know where it went.

One final note of personal interest is that my paternal grandparents and their daughter, my Aunt Mary Fiddes, who died in childbirth, were among the last to be buried there. Perhaps this explains why I feel that I have a special link with St Fittick's church.

Lizzie Finlayso

Unforgettable fire

When I was shown around Aberdeen Grammar school with the rest of my primary seven class, I had no idea that the pride of the building, the library and its Byronic relics, would shortly become a pile of cinders.

I have only a vague memory of being escorted around the library: it seemed very grand, with fluted columns supporting an upper gallery, where senior pupils sat studying, passing the odd sneer down towards us. 'The next time you come here' said Mr Will the art teacher, 'you'll be pupils of Aberdeen Grammar school'.

This statement was put into question one day in July in the late morning as, coming home from one of my last days at Mile End Primary school, I heard the scream of fire engine sirens in the streets heading towards the Grammar. On the television, news was breaking that the school was on fire. We saw images of flames sweeping across the top of the distinctive 1863 building, the statue of Lord Byron impassive to the heat behind him. The cause was, it seems, due to a workman leaving his paint stripper unattended for a moment, which caught fire to a curtain and spread rapidly. On my first visit, I had been impressed with the outer façade of the building as well as the inner: there were old chimney vents shaped like turrets, which excited my imagination, thinking of it as a castle. In the real world, however, these vents were far from practical, and only helped spread the fire.

A quarter of the school in all was gutted when the fire was at last put out, right in its metaphorical and physical heart. There was talk as to whether the school could continue. By the end of the summer holidays, we knew it would do so, in the form of portacabins hastily erected on the front lawn to replace the burnt out classrooms.

Starting secondary school in such a location hardly seemed very promising compared to the historic grandeur of the old library. Our first day in general seemed a bit chaotic. We first years filed past the set of gates opening onto Whitehall Place at the rear of the school. The other set of gates opening onto that street were locked, leading as they did to one of the burnt parts. The roofless

shell looked forlorn, its windows glass-less and glaring.

Most of the portacabins were substitute English classrooms, given the proximity of these rooms to the old library. The substitute library did not amount to much either, being a ragtag collection of singed paperbacks arranged at the back of the assembly hall. This venue proved quite unsuitable for serious study, as the library's main function clashed with various other events better suited to the hall.

Erecting the portacabins as a provisional measure showed a commitment to restoring the school, yet nothing seemed to change the course of our first three years. Men in hard hats came and went, pointing up at the scaffolding and waving plans about. I envied them their access to the site, which understandably remained out of bounds to

School days were happy days!

the pupils. The history of that part of the school had gripped me the one time I saw it intact, and continued to do so now it was dead and gone. Our guidance teacher's room was situated in the older part of the main building, with a view of the burnt part below, to the left. I used to look down in solitary fascination.

Once, at the end of my third year, in June 1989, when the school scripture union organized a trip out to Balmedie Beach, I had the chance to see a burnt section up close when the mini-bus we were to travel in was parked there. I went up to the still scorched stone to look at the inside. The forbidding, blackened mass with loss written all over it was attractive to me in a morbid sort of way. This was the second entrance onto Whitehall Place, nearest Esslemont Avenue, the one normally locked, which I had glimpsed on my first day.

In our fourth year, the re-building finally begun. We were the first pupils in our school to take Standard Grade exams, labelled as guinea pigs in this area more than once. Increasingly, the sounds of hammering, drilling and all manner of clanking machinery were heard inside the restricted zone, but there was little immediate effect on the outside. We plugged our ears over in the language block, and continued to pour over French verbs.

Ironically, considering we had not had the benefits of the old school either, the restorations were not completed until very shortly before we were due to leave, at the end of our sixth year. We occupy a unique place in the school's history as a result. In March 1992, a group of VIPs were shown around the school to be reassured that they'd been wise to invest in its reconstruction.

My modern studies class were taking part in an animated debate about the future NHS, which involved one character doing an amusing impression of Winston Churchill in defending the values of that estimable institution. However, the new building would not be opened properly until the next session, after we were gone.

On Monday 25 May, a friend and I went back to school to return our modern studies books, no longer in school uniform. We sat in the sixth-year common room and talked about our school days now past, some rather better than others. We went up to have a look at the new library, which was locked. The new shelves, with their new books were denied to us. With only a vague memory of what the 1986 library had been like. What our school days might have been without the fire, we will never know.

David Tallach

3 Aberdonian Allsorts: the great, the good, the seldom heard of

Graft and corruption
Prize Winning Entry

Misleading the public by telling lies. Playing on the fears and ignorance of the poor. Local dignitaries using council property for their own wicked purposes. This was the state of Aberdeen in the eighteenth century.

Their worst outrage was referred to as the 'Servant Trade' by the organizers of a money-making scheme which involved the kidnapping of little children and transporting them to North America, where they were sold into virtual slavery. The perpetrators of this abuse were the City Fathers, the councillors and bailies of Aberdeen. From 1740 to 1746 partnerships were formed, not only in Aberdeen, but also in other towns in Scotland to carry out this disgraceful practice. Among the guilty men were Bailie William Fordyce of Aquhorthies; Walter Cochran the Town Clerk depute and several other persons of note and fortune in the city.

They employed bands of scoundrels to tour the town and surrounding countryside, luring the unwary with promises of a marvellous life in the New World. Plying some with drink and others with bribes - anything to get them to make their mark and sign up for what was to be a one-way ticket to the plantations in America. Because of the terrible famine of 1740 the people were so poor that some were persuaded to sell their offspring to these companies and the account books have entries such as: 'To Robert Ross, for listing his son, one shilling'; and 'To W. MacLean, for listing his brother Donald, one shilling and sixpence'.

However, most of their victims were press-ganged or kidnapped by the villains, who hunted down and snatched unwary children whom they thought fit for their purpose. The unfortunates were herded through the streets like cattle and housed in a barn by the Green. There they would be kept until a ship was ready to sail across the Atlantic. If the barn became overcrowded then the overflow would be lodged in the workhouse or even in the Tollbooth, the town prison.

It is hard to imagine that the citizens of Aberdeen would allow such things to occur, but they were ignorant of their rights and easily cowed into submission by those in authority. Helpless mothers followed the victims as they were marched down to the harbour calling out piteous farewells to their children and cursing their captors. Those who attempted rescue were restrained and threatened with jail.

One can only imagine the atrocious conditions of the voyage across the Atlantic that those children would have had to endure; a voyage that would have lasted months. Once in America they were auctioned off to the highest bidder as bonded servants for five or seven years. The planters they were sold to frequently treated them harshly, and if they ran off and were at liberty for thirty days, another year was added to their bondage.

This horrifying episode in Aberdeen's history might have slipped into obscurity and been forgotten about if it had not been for Peter Williamson - the man who returned. Peter was born at Hirnley in the parish of Aboyne in 1730. At the age of eleven while on a visit to Aberdeen he was enticed aboard the *Kenilworth* and thrown into a hold already packed with children. The vessel then set sail on a voyage that was to last for eleven weeks.

The *Kenilworth* had almost reached its destination when disaster struck. In a violent storm it struck a sandbank off Cape May near to the Cape of Delaware. Fearing that the ship would sink the cowardly crew took to the boats leaving the cargo of children to go down with the ship. However it remained grounded on the sandbank and the children were rescued by another ship and taken to Philadelphia.

In Philadelphia, the city of brotherly love, the children were auctioned off for about sixteen pounds a head. Here Peter had a stroke of luck for he was bonded to a Hugh Wilson for seven years. This man had been a bonded servant himself and he treated Peter well. He was given light work to do and during the winter when work was slack Peter went to school. When he was fourteen and fit for harder work Peter did his fair share of work on the farm and served his master well.

In 1757, when Peter was seventeen and still had two years of his bondage to serve, Hugh Wilson died. In his will Hugh Wilson had granted Peter his freedom, left him £200, his best horse and saddle and all his wearing apparel.

For the next seven years Peter did jobbing work around and about. Then he married the daughter of a rich planter. His father-in-law gave Peter the deeds to a tract of land that lay

on the frontiers of the province of Pennsylvania. There were 200 acres, thirty of which were cleared. He was doing better than ever he would have in Scotland.

All went well for a year when once again disaster struck. The French had designs on the territory and stirred up the Indians by offering them £15 sterling for every British scalp they took. In October of 1754, while his wife was away visiting relatives, a band of Indians attacked Peter's farm and captured him. Because he was of a sturdy build, instead of killing him they used him as a beast of burden to carry their booty.

He had to endure the horror of seeing neighbouring farms attacked, their occupants killed outright or tortured to death and the buildings being burned down. For three months he was a captive of the Indians until he managed to escape. When he returned to his father-in-law he found that his wife had taken ill and died.

Peter then joined the British army to help fight against the French and their Indian allies. After being wounded he was captured by the French and taken to Quebec. There was an exchange of prisoners of war and Peter was shipped back to Plymouth where he was discharged as unfit for further service. As he only had a small amount of money he decided that he would walk back to Aberdeen. By the time he got to York he was penniless but a small group of gentlemen heard his story and provided enough money for him to publish a pamphlet giving an account of how he was kidnapped and sold as a slave in the New World, and of his subsequent adventures there. Dressed in the garb of a Cherokee warrior - souvenirs he had brought back with him- Peter attracted crowds of onlookers in the various villages and towns on his way north. By selling his pamphlet to the curious he made enough money to make his way back to Aberdeen.

Although it was sixteen years since he had been kidnapped, the men responsible were still in power. When they read the pamphlet he was selling to the citizens of Aberdeen the guilty men were incensed, and had Peter arrested for libel and charged with defaming the character and reputation of the merchants of Aberdeen.

He was brought before two of the bailies and pleaded in vain that the sufferings he had endured should mitigate the charges against him. He was convicted of libel and the offending pages torn from the book and burned by the public hangman at the market cross. He was then imprisoned until he agreed to crave the pardon of the magistrates in the most submissive manner. He was then fined ten shillings and banished from the town.

After this humiliating experience Peter went to Edinburgh, where enlightened humanitarians took up his case and it was brought to the notice of judges of the Supreme Court. So in 1762 a unanimous judgement was found in Peter's favour,

condemning the provost of Aberdeen, four bailies, and the dean of the guild jointly. Peter received £100 for being imprisoned in the Tolbooth on his return to Aberdeen in 1758.

Returning to Edinburgh Peter was determined to seek justice for his kidnapping as a boy in 1741, and so began proceedings against Bailie William Fordyce. It took another six years but once again judgement was found in Peter's favour, but before he could collect the £200 awarded to him the Bailie conveniently died. Strange to relate, when the Bailie's widow died and they were burying her beside her late husband, it was decided to have a look at him. When they opened his coffin they found that all it contained were some granite blocks about the same weight as a man. What had become of William Fordyce? Whether he had really died or simply disappeared remains a mystery to this day.

As for Peter Williamson - the man who returned - he became a kenspeckle figure in

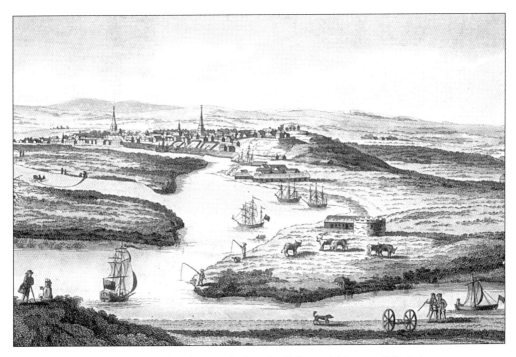

Aberdeen harbour, from here the bondage began. (Aberdeen Art Gallery and Museums Collection)

Edinburgh where he settled and opened an inn, where he entertained his customers with tales of his adventures in the New World. Ever the enterprising man, he published the first street directory of Edinburgh and then went on to establish the first postal service in the town.

R. J. Arthur

Old soldiers never die

James Mathieson was my grandfather; my memory of him is sitting in his armchair by the fireside, smoking his pipe, a very quiet man, except when he was chastising the grandchildren or dog, in Urdu! His black and white mongrel bitch was called 'Lady' after Ladysmith in South Africa.

When my grandfather died in 1947 my father was abroad in the Merchant Navy; my grandmother decreed, as I was the eldest son

of the eldest son, I was to be the senior mourner. At the tender age of five and a half, there I was in my short trousers and school cap at the head of the column of bowler-hatted and be-medalled veterans from the Gordon Highlanders club and the Aberdeen branch of the South Africa War Veterans Association.

The funeral notice stated, 'assemble at the cemetery gates', but despite their advanced years the old soldiers walked the one mile from the house along the Hardgate to Allenvale Cemetery, the cortege followed the hearse, the only sound the clinking of medals. My earliest memory is of one elderly veteran towering over me, he was exceptionally tall and extremely gaunt, and he took it upon himself to look after me.

Fifty years on, in June 1999 my interest was aroused by an article in the *Evening Express* contributed by Mrs Harriet Ellis. Her father Alexander Sutherland Innes was president and

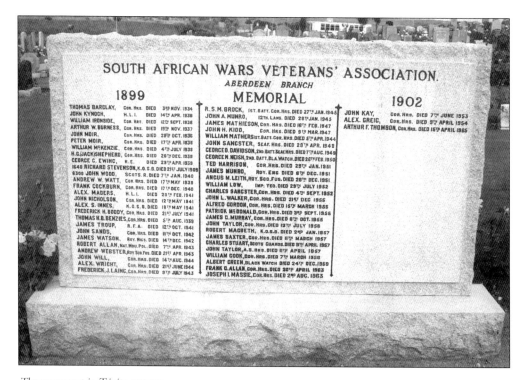

The monument in Trinity cemetery.

one of the founders of the Aberdeen branch of the SAWVA. Alexander Innes was a very public spirited man, he felt there should be a permanent reminder of the men who served in South Africa and was the inspiration behind a very impressive memorial located in Trinity Cemetery South. The monument sits on the slope of the Broad Hill with Pittodrie Stadium as a backdrop. This is not a war memorial commemorating the fallen, instead the little known memorial records some of the local men who served during the Boer War 1899 to 1902 and returned, most of them to live on to a ripe old age, my grandfather James Mathieson is included on the headstone.

The newspaper article was accompanied by a photograph; taken on the parade ground at the Bridge of Don Barracks during an open day in 1936, the year after the new depot opened. The photo includes my grandfather James Mathieson, also the tall gentleman who took me under his wing at my grandad's funeral. Subsequent research revealed my 'minder' was one Angus Stuart, he had served on the North West Frontier and took part in the action at Dargai where Piper Findlater won his Victoria Cross. The picture shows Alexander Innes sitting proudly in the front row surrounded by a grand body of men, almost half of whom are wearing medals from the First World War.

At the beginning of the war in South Africa the British Army suffered a number of defeats referred to as 'The Black Week'. Scotland grieved at the losses of the Highland Brigade at Magersfontein. No one realised that just twelve years after the end of the Boer War those losses were to be overwhelmed by the casualties during the First World War. Despite having suffered the horror and hardships of the trenches the memories of these men went back further to their time in South Africa. A different war, endless trekking across the veldt in all weathers, from baking heat and not enough water to drink, to torrential rain,

hailstorms and mud that literally saw mules and oxen drop in their tracks. At times, being on half rations was a luxury.

In those days they were a different breed of men, loyal to Queen and Country. During an advance a column stopped for the night, the priority was to find sufficient firewood, if only enough to boil water. It was Queen Victoria's birthday and while the troops were scratching around for kindling one of the soldiers started to sing 'God Save The Queen,' in no time hundreds of voices had joined in the National Anthem. Truly 'Soldiers of the Queen'.

Along with the rest of the branches, as the old soldiers 'faded away' the records, membership details, minutes of committee meetings etc. were lost. I succeeded in discovering a fair amount concerning a number of the members and went on to identify a further twenty-one of the individuals in the photograph. My research was totally absorbing; the most rewarding part was locating and talking to descendants of the veterans.

Mrs Laura Geddes, the daughter of James Balfour, keeps her father's memory alive; his medals are proudly on display, also an outstanding collection of photographs mainly of his service in India have survived.

James Balfour, enlisted in the 2nd Battalion Gordon Highlanders in 1898, served in South Africa and India, he was a regimental boxing champion. First World War service was in France with the 24th Battalion, a Territorial unit, he also served with the London Scottish and went on to become a Company Sergeant Major, he qualified for the Territorial Force War Medal, a comparatively rare award.

When the Great War ended Sgt Major Balfour remained behind with the Army of Occupation and did not return to Aberdeen till 1920 when he found to his cost that 'Dear Old Blighty' was not a 'Land fit for heroes', by that time any jobs that had been available were long gone. The treatment he received led him to take an interest in local politics and he became a well-known town councillor and the inspiration behind the first thrift shop in Aberdeen.

By all accounts James Balfour was a bit of a character; people of that generation made their own entertainment, singing, recitals, performing various displays etc. Laura Geddes recalls attending the meetings in Mearns Street which were also a social evening, including wives and children. A number of the relatives of the veterans commented their fathers endured hard times in later life, for some entertainment at the Seaman's Mission was their only opportunity for an evening out.

John Alexander Munro, served with the 12th Royal Lancers, he was groom to the commanding officer Lord Airlie. On 11 June 1900 at Diamond Hill, east of Pretoria, Lord Airlie was killed and John Munro wounded.

John Munro was awarded five clasps to his Queen's South Africa medal and went on to serve in India. John was a stalwart of the association and the standard bearer on parade. His daughter Christina Dorward has proud memories of the association and her father, and recalls him polishing his shoes before every parade as if he were still in the cavalry.

The association church was the 'Mither Kirk', the West Kirk of St Nicholas, the association padre was the Reverend P.C. Millar. A photograph exists of the veterans entering the churchyard from Backwynd, with Shirrais Laing's shop in the background.

By 1971 membership of the association was declining due to the old soldiers fading away, the association was 'stood down' at a ceremony in the grounds of the Royal Hospital Chelsea. 1983 saw the last roll call countrywide, a total of six veterans. The youngest, at ninety-eight,

Bridge of Don Barracks, 1936.

William Center meets Prince Charles.

John Munro in uniform of the 5th Royal Irish Lancers.

was a local man, William Center. William served in Peshwar, India 1905 or 1906, was subsequently discharged to the Reserve and recalled to the 'Colours' at the outbreak of the First World War.

William, now in the 1st Battalion, was wounded at the end of August 1914, and due to the 'Fog of War' was captured along with most of his comrades. He spent almost the entire war as a prisoner of the Germans. On repatriation he used his accumulated back pay to buy a piece of land and installed his mother and sister on a half-acre croft near Udny.

On 4 October 1980 William attended a rally of Gordon Highlanders past and present at Crathes Castle near Banchory. William's son has a photograph of his father shaking hands with Prince Charles; to think William Center had served the 'Old Queen' at the turn of the century and there he was chatting with her great, great, great grandson.

William Center, Peshawar, India.

James Balfour, extreme left.

William died on 27 February 1984 aged ninety-eight, just short of Ladysmith Day. A funeral party from his old regiment carried his coffin across the Green to the graveside at Udny Church.

Aberdeen is very privileged to be home to such a unique memorial, to the best of my knowledge it is the only one of its kind in the UK. The memorial is not only a monument but fourteen of the veterans chose to be buried there; they served together far from home and now lie at rest together. The association represented a fine example of comradeship and an intense loyalty between a group of men with shared memories.

'Old Soldiers never die, they simply fade away. '

John W. Mathieson

Souter Willie

It was in Aberdeen in 1771 and Willie Taylor sat in his garret stitching away with waxed thread. He was in a good mood, he had just been made a Burgess of the town and as befits a Burgess he had taken larger premises. It was not to be a big move, only across the road in fact, but the change in status was immense. At the end of the month he and Elspet Duncan, his wife of just a few weeks, would be moving and the future looked bright.

William was not the first Taylor in the Spital. His grandfather John, also a souter, had been granted a sasine there in 1725, but had sold it in the 1750s and moved out. Now the family name was returning and Willie felt rather proud of his achievement.

He stood up to stretch his legs and coughed. The cough would not go away

The family in 1910.

despite all the cures the apothecary recom-
mended. Perhaps he would be able to take it a
little more easy now he was a burgess, after all
he would now be able to have an apprentice.
He would also be able to take the air with
Elspet in the Castlegate, which was the place
to be seen.

So William Taylor Esq., Burgess of the City
of Aberdeen, and his wife moved across the
road, and for a few months all went well. He
even took on an apprentice under the usual
terms:

'apprenticed to William Taylor, shoemaker
for five years from date. The father to give a
bedding of clothes and maintain him in board
and diet for the first half-year and provide
wearing clothes during the whole space. Master
to maintain him in bed and board during the
remaining time and a pair of shoes yearly'.

Towards the end of the year Elspet announced that she was expecting and it seemed
that their happiness was complete. The one
cloud on the horizon was his cough, which
became worse during the winter, and though
he tried everything it was all to no avail. The
summer came without any relief, though he
was quite cheerful in July when his son John
was born. He became so worried, in fact, that
he sought permission to have his son entered
on the roll of burgesses, as he was entitled to
do, and put his affairs in order, leaving his wife
and son in the care of his father. Sadly his
premonition was justified and he died on 1
November. He was buried in the Spital and
the family had to start all over again.

John was baptised in St Nicholas in 1772
and grew up in his grandfather's house with
his mother. He became an apprentice
shoemaker to his grandfather, and was
indentured for five years, not the usual seven,

James and Fred.

James and Margaret, 1948.

as he was the son of a burgess. By the time he was twenty-six he had his own business. Looking for premises he saw a notice in the local paper which offered 'house and ground-dry and airy' in the Spital, but couldn't afford the asking price and looked for something cheaper.

A report in the news section said that the recent storms had thrown many firkins of butter up on the shore. And nearer home, Thomas and James Henderson, father and son, shoemakers were said to have 'purloined some leather and were supposed to be gone by the way of Inverness' created something of a stir in the trade. There was much talk of tightening up the system and for a while shoemakers were regarded with some suspicion.

However the fuss had died down by the time he married Janet Tiviotdale on 11 March 1804 in Old Machar. She came from an old Insch family, though she had ancestors from Caithness going back as far as 1664. They had a son, John, baptised on 23 March 1811 at St Nicholas, who worked at his father's trade, and established quite a reputation. When he was about twenty he fell in love with the daughter of a rival shoemaker (and a Burgess to boot!) They were married in St Nicholas on the 31 December 1833, and decided it was best to leave Aberdeen and start afresh in Dundee.

There was plenty of work for a shoemaker there and he did well. They had a large family, one of whom, James Moir born in 1848 married Charlotte Duthie in 1871. The Duthies came from Aberdeen, her father was married at St Nicholas on 24 November 1843, so the two families had a lot in common.

James did not follow his father's trade but instead became a house painter. He became a journeyman and Charlotte was a drawing frame worker in the local jute mill. Within a year of their marriage they returned to Aberdeen. There they rented a flat in Gilcomston Terrace, where eventually their five children were born. First came Frederick in 1872, followed by Charles, Annie, Jessie and finally James Moir in 1876.

This year was remarkable in other ways too. In April, a ferryboat sank in the Dee with the loss of forty lives, prompting demands for a bridge to be built – later to be Victoria Bridge. Then just before Christmas, a storm blew up which broke the retaining chains on the lock gate of the harbour.

The children grew up with change all around them. In 1879 a Mr Tulloch submitted plans for a flight of steps linking Crown Street with Bridge Street, and in 1886 work began on Rosemount Viaduct. But there were other sights to fascinate a youngster as well. In particular the Gordon Highlanders in their Castlegate barracks, and on 2 February 1892, twenty-year-old Frederick joined them. James could hardly bear to wait until he could follow his brother, but at last in 1894, when he was just eighteen, he did so and began a whole new chapter in his life.

So James Taylor joined the Gordons and, after basic training, he was included in a draft to India to join the 1st Battalion. The train journey from Aberdeen to Glasgow and on to Liverpool was an exciting adventure for a lad who had never left Aberdeen. But it was nothing compared to boarding the troopship *Nubia*. Conditions on troopships at that time were primitive, with cramped accommodation and poor food, but it was all new and fascinating. They landed at Karachi and immediately marched to Umballa, the battalion's headquarters. Although he had lost his Aberdeen pallor by the time he had arrived, he and his mates were still very raw recruits and the large draft had to be spread round the battalion to ensure continued efficiency. Here he was reunited with brother Fred and spent many hours exchanging news and experiences.

After a short break the reinforced battalion then marched to Rawalpindi, 367 miles across

James (right) in later years as a 'postie'.

the almost trackless countryside. They were there for a week or two before marching a further 137 miles to Lahore to take part in the Vice-Regal Durbar, a tough initiation for raw recruits with only a few months service. The routine on the march was always the same – an early start, well before sun-up ensured, even with 'coffee breaks', that they reached their camping ground by 11 a.m. They rested for the remainder of the day, at liberty to write letters, or even swim if there was a nearby river, until the evening meal. It was then early to bed, ready for the next day's sweltering march.

During his sojourn in India, James found himself in the thick of the Gordon's attack on Tirah, the battalion found itself under fire at Dargai, overlooking the route they were taking. The Gordons were in the lead at this point and, setting off at 5 a.m. on the 18 October, were under fire as they began to climb to get into position to attack. By 2 p.m. on the 20 October they were ready and according to the official history,

'went straight up the hill without check or hesitation headed by their pipers. This splendid battalion marched across the open ground, through murderous fire and in forty minutes won the heights, leaving three officers and thirty men killed or wounded on the way. The first rush of the Gordons was deserving of the highest praise, for they had just undergone a very severe climb and had reached a point beyond which other troops had been unable to advance – few of the enemy waited for bayonet'.

The advance reached the sheltering rocks, officers waving their swords to those behind, and Piper Findlater of the Gordons, though wounded in both feet, sat under heavy fire playing the regimental march to encourage them. Piper Findlater, who incidentally came from Turriff, was awarded the VC for his actions during the battle. James Taylor and his brother, were awarded the clasp 'Tirah 1897/98' to the India Medal of 1896.

Conditions were bad. After freezing nights they would breakfast in pouring rain and then have to advance under fire, often across snow swollen rivers up to their waists in icy water. Taming the truculent tribes took three months of hard campaigning, but eventually British rule was re-established and the battalion marched down and entrained for Peshawar. In all operations twenty-four officers and some 600 men had been killed or wounded. James Taylor received the 'Punjab Frontier 1897/8' clasp to the India Medal for his privations on the sub-continent.

It was time to go home at last and the great day arrived. They entrained for Deolali and Bombay and embarked on their old friend the P & O transport *Nubia*. They eventually took passage home on the SS *Menes*, via Malta and Gibraltar to Liverpool. When they arrived home they were treated like heroes, marching through the streets and being entertained to a civic reception including an 'excellent repast' in the town hall.

They were not to rest on their laurels for long. Barely a year passed before the call of Empire came again, this time to South Africa. At the Orange River Station, James was wounded in the chest. He spent most of the following year in hospital and was eventually discharged wounded in 1900. His one regret was that he was unable to perform the gymnastics for which he was renowned in the regiment, but by far the biggest regret was having to leave the regiment he loved before his time was up. So at the age of twenty-four, with a small pension in his pocket he had to start afresh.

The railways were booming, so he started as a porter at Aberdeen Joint Station, but soon became a postman instead. He worked in various parts of Aberdeenshire, and it was while he was at Peterhead that he met Margaret McRae, daughter of the meal miller at Caies Mill, Dyce. She could trace her line back to the Black Isle in 1775, and her parents

were married in Forres on 17 June 1874, after which they came to Dyce. James would often cycle from his lodgings at Hatton of Fintray to Dyce to spend an hour or two with Margaret, and when her father moved to Little Mill at Newhills he was even closer. On special occasions they would often spend the day in Aberdeen, and one such was in the February before they were married, when they visited, by corporation tram, the stranded steamer James Hall which had run aground on Aberdeen Beach.

They were married on 29 April 1904 at Richmond Café. Correction Wynd and lived at Blackburn near Margaret's parents for a while. They had their first child, Mary Ann, there, later moving to Kinaldie and then Turriff. The family grew with the addition of James, Roderick, Charles (who died aged nine months) and Edith. The year Edith was born is long remembered in Turriff. It was the year of the 'Turra Coo.' A local farmer refused to pay the new National Insurance for his men and one of his cows was poinded for public auction. It proved impossible to sell, but the event seized the public imagination, and souvenir pottery, poems and jingles were produced to mark the event.

Then the First World War broke out in 1914 and James couldn't wait to get into uniform again. This time he was in the Scottish Horse, a training regiment based in Fife and it was here that a daughter, Margaret, was born. At thirty-eight and in poor health, he served out the rest of the war in Fife, and was awarded the General Service Medal at the end of his service.

James resumed his postal duties in Turriff and with the birth of another daughter, Ann Graham, the family was complete. He joined the British Legion and became a member of the famous Turriff Silver Band, but sorrow struck in 1921 when James, his eldest son, just fifteen, was fatally injured in a road accident. He was happy enough in Turriff, with the town providing all they needed. In the High Street, Annie Hays General Store, with nearby Stewart's Grocers and in the Square, Carnegie the butcher. For himself there was Milnes Boot and Shoe Shop for his 'posties' boots.

He retired in 1936, but still kept busy, becoming Beadle of the church and gardener for the manse, and with the outbreak of war in 1939 saw service in the Civil Defence. He died in 1957, and is buried in Turriff Cemetery next to his beloved Maggie.

J. Trevor Jenkins

The surgical scientist of Union Street

The site of 252 Union Street is now occupied by a block of offices erected about 1933, but the Victorian dwelling demolished to make way for it was, for over fifty years, the home of Sir Alexander Ogston. The site of his garden is now a car park and there is no trace of the building which once stood there, which served as Ogston's laboratory, and where in 1879 he made a major scientific discovery. The life of this pioneering surgeon presents a remarkable story.

Alex Ogston was born in 1844, and he graduated in medicine at Aberdeen University in 1865, at the early age of twenty-one. He had already spent a year visiting medical clinics in Austria, Germany and Switzerland, during which he became fluent in German, and made a special study of ophthalmic surgery. After a short period in general practice he opened an eye dispensary in the city in 1866, which led to his appointment as Ophthalmic Surgeon to the Royal Infirmary in 1868. Then, in 1870, aged twenty-six, he joined the surgical staff as Assistant Surgeon.

The infirmary building in which Ogston worked still stands, outwardly unchanged, at

The infirmary at Woolmanhill.

Woolmanhill. It was designed by Archibald Simpson, the architect of the Music Hall and the Triple Kirks, and was opened in 1840. Ogston later recalled the conditions he knew as a student:

'the wards, even the corridors, stank with the mawkish odour of suppuration, and not a single wound healed without festering. Each stuffy ward was presided over by an old woman, whose only qualification was her ability to make a poultice. In the staff room there hung a row of old black coats covered with the dirt of years and encrusted with blood stains. These were donned by surgeons before going to the operating theatre. Here there was no apparatus for washing the hands, on a shelf lay the instruments open for anyone to handle, and suture needles were stuck in a jampot of rancid lard. Small wonder that our operation wounds suppurated'.

Today the building is clean and quiet, and one can climb the main staircase and stand beside the narrow door leading into the operating theatre, which lay beneath the dome of the building. In 1840 there was no general anaesthesia, so few patients could face the terror of an operation: surgeons could only operate when pain and disability had made the sufferer desperate for relief. Consequently, in 1844, only 100 operations were performed – about two each week. One can hardly imagine the scene when a terrified boy with a bladder stone, or a woman facing mastectomy, was carried through the door into the noisy amphitheatre. The students, sitting in tiered rows, chattered and stared as the patient was bound to the blood-stained operating table. To the awful immediate prospect of unbearable pain, there was for both patients and surgeon the very real threat that post-operative sepsis would deny them both a useful result.

By the 1860s, when Ogston was a student, the use of ether and chloroform had mercifully become established (Ogston acted as Assistant Anaesthetist during 1871). Theatre routines were, however, largely unchanged and Ogston recalled how,,

'after every operation we used to await with trembling the dreaded third day, when sepsis set in; experience had taught us the danger of that critical time, but we were in utter ignorance of how to avoid it.'

Then, in 1867, Professor Joseph Lister in Glasgow, inspired by the work of Louis Pasteur, published his first papers on the antiseptic principle in the practice of surgery. 'Unforgettable,' recalled Ogston, 'was the incredulity with which we heard the first announcement that Lister had discovered a means of avoiding suppuration in operation wounds'. (Perhaps this made a particular impression on Ogston with his experience of eye operations). He decided to see for himself, and in late 1869 he travelled to Glasgow. Lister had just left his position there to return to Edinburgh as Professor of Clinical Surgery, so Ogston went to see the Listerian work in the hands of his former assistant and successor, Hector Cameron.

'He took me to his wards. Five minutes later found me convinced of the truth of the marvellous discovery. I was shown a knee joint which had been opened. There could be no room for doubt. The wound into the joint was there, but where was the inflammation that ought fatally to have followed? The limb was perfectly well, the wound clean and healing. I saw that a marvellous change had come over our science. From that time we introduced the methods of Lister into the wards. All the surgical instruments were immersed in 1 in 20 carbolic lotion, the hands of the surgical team were thoroughly washed

Stair to the original theatre.

and rinsed in the lotion, and all drapes and swabs were soaked in it. The managers of the infirmary complained of the expense of providing clean dressings and fresh carbolic lotion for every patient.'

The older members of the staff were indifferent if not actively hostile to Ogston's practice. Nevertheless, in 1870 he was appointed an Assistant Surgeon.

Ogston found that relatively little work came his way – in 1874 there were still fewer than 100 general surgical operations performed in a year, and consequently surgeons generally found their livelihood in general practice. For Ogston this was soon to change. In 1874 he became Full Surgeon, and immediately the number of operations rose, for he was confident that, by taking full antiseptic precautions, it was safe for him to extend the range of operations among the 1,100-1,200 surgical patients admitted each year.

Surgery in the nineteenth century.

In 1876, on 17 May, he performed what soon became known as Ogston's operation. At that time poor diet and living conditions had made knock knees and bowed legs due to rickets a common complaint among young people attending the hospital. For this trial Ogston chose a youth of eighteen, a moulder in the iron works, who from the age of six had noticed progressive knock-knee deformity, severely limiting his mobility. The operation involved opening the knee joint, dividing bone with a chisel, and manipulating the leg straight, with splintage for several weeks. Ogston must have watched the progress of this first deliberate opening of a knee joint with considerable anxiety because, before Lister, such a procedure would have been universally condemned. Although the operation had been performed 'with a minute observance of Lister's antiseptic precautions', it had still been done in a dusty ill-ventilated theatre, crowded with students, and regularly used by surgeons who continued to operate in the old un-sterile manner. The wound healed without event. On 6 June the other knee was similarly treated, and by mid-July the patient was walking on two straight legs. Ogston reported this operation to the German Surgical Society in 1877 and soon the operation was being performed regularly in many European centres: it was one of the first open operations on a joint to be reported.

By 1878 operations on bones and joints were being performed regularly, and Ogston was reflecting on the real reason which lay behind the safe operating conditions conferred by the antiseptic regime. Lister was still vague on this subject, but Ogston was becoming convinced that one or more special germs were responsible for surgical sepsis, and were destroyed by carbolisation of everything which came in contact with the operation wound. One day in 1879 his thoughts led him, after he had drained an acute abscess, to take a sample of the pus to his home, where he stained a film with aniline violet, as had been suggested by Robert Koch, and placed the slide under his student's microscope.

'My delight may be conceived when there were revealed beautiful tangles, tufts and chains of round organisms (micrococci) in great numbers, distinct among the pus cells.'

Ogston obtained a grant to buy a microscope from Zeiss of Jena, with an oil-immersion lens, and went on to examine the pus from every abscess drained in the infirmary: micrococci were found in the pus from every acute abscess.

He then had a small laboratory built in his garden, installed an incubator and cages for small animals, and obtained a licence allowing experimentation on mice and guinea-pigs. When a drop of pus from an acute abscess was injected under the skin of a mouse it became ill, micrococci were found in its blood, and an abscess grew at the site of the injection. Then, in the most original part of these experiments, Ogston attempted to grow the micrococci in pure culture. This was uncharted territory, but he hit on the idea of incubating pus in newly-laid eggs. One minim of pus was injected, with sterile precautions, into the albumen and the egg incubated at 98 Fahrenheit for ten days. When the egg was opened 'the albumen was filled with enormous chains or masses of micrococci, a drop of this albumen injected into an animal's back now produced a typical abscess'. When the micrococci lay in chains (already named streptococci by Billroth) the infection produced was severe: when the cocci grew in clumps like grapes injection of the culture usually produced an acute localised abscess.

When Ogston reported these findings to his colleagues in Aberdeen he was met with disbelief, but when he addressed the annual congress of the German Surgical Society in Berlin in 1880 he was received with acclamation. He reported to the Grants Committee of the British Medical Association, which had assisted in setting up his laboratory, and it is a remarkable document. The work had been done in a garden hut, by a general surgeon without assistance, at a time when there was only a handful of bacteriology laboratories in existence. He wrote as an experienced pathologist, and laid down the rules for proving that a specific germ is responsible for a particular disease, for example the germ obtained from pus or blood taken from a diseased patient must first be isolated, and grown in pure culture: this was injected into a healthy animal, and the original disease produced. This was several years before these rules were enunciated by the more experienced bacteriologist, Robert Koch, in Berlin. With the help of the Professor of Greek, Ogston named the cocci growing in clusters like grapes *staphylococci*, and because their colonies on culture were bright yellow

the full name was *Staphylococcus aureus*. It remains the main cause of acute suppuration. At this time, in the early 1880s, there were still only 150-200 operations being performed each year. In 1882 Ogston was appointed Regius Professor of Surgery, and by 1888 over 500 operations were carried out in the year, 350 by Ogston himself. Most significantly, the abdomen was for the first time being opened, and ten women with large ovarian cysts were freed from this encumbrance.

Soon the wards in the Simpson building were overcrowded, and during the 1890s the surgical block backing onto Spa Street was built and opened in 1892, while the medical block on Woolmanhill was completed in 1897. A new operating theatre in the basement of the surgical block was still an amphitheatre seating 200 students, but it was served by a lift and had scrub-up sinks, instrument boilers and an autoclave for sterilising theatre linen. (Even so, operating could not commence until the daily surgical

The dome, beneath which the original theatre lay.

lecture had been delivered in the same amphitheatre). The students valued Ogston's clear and memorable lectures, and his bedside teaching was characterised by particular consideration for the feelings of the patients, and the detailed physical examination he always practised. This was in fact essential because - apart from blood counts - it was the sole source of information. Peptic ulceration and gallstones were quite common, but there was no way of demonstrating them except by clinical examination. Ogston led the way in operating for emergencies such as perforation of a gastric ulcer, intestinal obstruction, and ectopic pregnancy, and in widening the scope of elective operations on the gall bladder, kidneys and ureters.

When Ogston retired, after thirty years on the staff of the infirmary, the number of operations performed was 930, but only in about thirty was the abdomen opened. In the following year the first operation for acute appendicitis was performed in Aberdeen, and thereafter the number of abdominal operations rose rapidly.

Ogston had an active retirement. He had a close interest in military surgery, and in the 1880s he visited France, Germany and Russia to study their medical services for their forces, and he concluded that they were much better prepared for active service than the United Kingdom. In an address to the British Medical Association in 1899 he drew forceful attention to these deficiencies. Within a year the Boer War had broken out and in June 1900, with the blessing of Queen Victoria, he visited South Africa. He found a very worrying situation, with thousands of British soldiers stricken with typhoid fever, receiving only the most primitive care, lying in tents on the bare ground on cold nights, attended by orderlies who knew nothing of sick nursing. Battle casualties were being evacuated in great discomfort in ox carts, and surgical care was inadequate. Ogston succumbed to typhoid

Sir Alexander Ogston.

fever, which was resulting in a score or so of deaths each day among the troops, and came very close to death himself. He paid warm tribute to the few overworked British nursing sisters, but was greatly disturbed by the dilatory attitude of senior army medical staff.

On his return home Ogston was appointed to the Committee of Experts set up to report on the future of Army Medicine, and some of his constructive criticisms bore fruit. Ogston was a tall and impressive figure, with high standards and expectations and an acute intelligence. This made him, like other pioneers, critical of those who could not appreciate advances in medicine even when they were presented with the evidence in their favour. But his patients and his students honoured him and, though he seemed austere, his family knew a loving and supportive parent, and his friendship once given was deeply valued.

It was appropriate that so positive and practical a man should end his active career at the age of seventy-two in the First World War. In August 1916 Ogston joined the first British Ambulance Unit in the Italian Alps, where he was the only surgeon with the Second Italian Army. Over fifteen months he operated, often under fire, through a winter of cold and damp, in miserable conditions, attending shell and grenade wounds and caring for many men with frostbite and trench foot. It may have been these privations which brought on severe rheumatism, which greatly restricted Ogston's activities until his death in 1929.

Peter Jones.

Kayaks on the Don

The modern town of Belhelvie is a pleasant place, much of it nice little granite faced modern houses nestled in coastal Aberdeenshire farmland. I'm certain that there are quicker routes down toward Balmedie and the sea than the one I took, redirected after a few false starts by helpful bus drivers and locals. But however uncertainly I wove my way towards the coast, I definitely fitted in better than a rather more exotic visitor to these climes around 270 years ago. It is his story which led me to this coastline on a sun soaked July day. In the top floor of Marischal college museum sit two kayaks (an Eskimo form of canoe) one of which has a curious story attached to it, perhaps best described by an entry in the 1824 catalogue of the Marischal College Museum: 'An Eskimaux canoe in which a native of that country was driven ashore near Belhelvie, about the beginning of the eighteenth century, and died soon after landing'

This particular kayak and the mystery of how it's pilot came to rest on the coastline of Aberdeenshire has puzzled scholars for quite literally centuries.

It seems that this particular Inuit was not alone in his visit to Scottish shores; in particular two rather happier occasions are recorded. Firstly that of Eenoolooapik a young Inuit brought to Aberdeen upon the whaling ship the *Neptune* by one Captain Penny in 1839, who returned to his homeland the following year by the same ship. This tale is recorded as a narrative in a book by Dr Alexander M'Donald, who served as a surgeon under Captain Penny. There has been some speculation that the kayak in Aberdeen's medico-chirurgical society is the one in which Dr M'Donald describes Eenoolooapik demonstrating his boating skills to locals upon the river Don. The second recorded case was that of Nouyabik, who arrived in Peterhead in May 1925; local records suggest that he became a great favourite with the locals and lived almost entirely off herring.

To return to the Belhelvie kayak, the earliest record of this kayak is in a transcript of the diary of one Reverend Francis Gastrell who made a tour of eastern Scotland in 1760 and recorded of his visit to Kings College, Old Aberdeen:

'In the church, which is not used (there being a Kirk for their way of worship) was a canoe about seven yards long by two feet wide, which, about thirty two years since, was driven into the Don with a man in it who was all over hairy and spoke a language which no person could there interpret. He lived but three days though all possible care was taken to recover him.'

The parish of Belhelvie.

The Belhelvie connection is mentioned by Francis Douglas in his *General description of the East coast of Scotland* published 1782 who mentions amongst the Marischal college collection:

'A canoe taken at sea with an Indian man in it about the beginning of this century. He was brought to Aberdeen, but died soon after his arrival and could give no account of himself. He is supposed to have lost his way at sea.'

It seems likely that these accounts refer to the same kayak, particularly in light of the fact that, at the time of Gastrell's visit, Kings College was (owing to the reformation) nothing more than a lumber-room and storage for odds and ends. Thus the kayak may have been transferred to Marischal by one of the professors without any record being made and this may explain the absence of such a record in the minutes.

Perhaps the more interesting questions are; where did this kayak come from? And how on earth did it and its unlikely pilot come to find himself off the shores of Aberdeenshire?

Earlier attempts to answer this riddle have often connected the kayak to the Baltic (particularly Norway, Finland and Lapland) however the kayak is clearly of Greenland origin and Professor Knud Rasmussen commented in an article on the Aberdeen kayaks in the 1930s, that no kayaks of the Greenland type had ever been used by any of the Baltic peoples. This seems to beg the question of how the kayaker and his vessel managed to cover the twelve hundred miles from Greenland to Scotland, particularly as a kayak becomes waterlogged and starts to sink if not dried out every forty-eight hours or so?

The generally accepted theory is that this Inuit was most likely taken captive by whalers and brought back as a curiosity, as is known to have been the case with some nine 'Eskimos' who had been taken to Denmark by different polar expeditions about the years 1640-47. This was also common enough in the Netherlands that in 1720 the Dutch States General passed a decree prohibiting the kidnapping of the natives of the Davis straight It is possible that the Belhelvie kayaker was taken captive by whalers and either escaped in

The coast at Balmedie, where an exotic visitor arrived.

his kayak when he saw land, or was set loose by the whalers, fearing some legal repercussions of their kidnapping.

However this is not the only recorded case of Inuit off the Scottish coast, as early as 1688 the Reverend James Wallace in his *Description of the Isles of Orkney* wrote:

'Sometime about this country are seen these men which are called Finn-Men; in the year 1682, one was seen sometime sailing rowing up and down in his little boat at the South end of the Isle of Eda, most of the people of the Isle flocked to see him, and when they adventured to put out a boat to see if they could apprehend him, he presently fled away most swiftly: And in the year 1864, another was seen from Westra, and for a while after they got few or no fishes; for they have a saying here that these Finnmen drive away the Fishes from the place to which they come.'

In a later edition, with additions made by his son, the *Description of the Isles of Orkney* connects these sightings to a kayak held in the Museum of Science and Art in Edinburgh (originally housed in the Physician's Hall) as well as one in the church of Burra in Orkney. This edition also includes a detailed description (presumably from one of the kayaks stored as a curiosity) and the theory that they belonged to inhabitants of the Davis straights.

Nor is this the only reported Inuit sighting dating from this period; Reverend John Brand writing in *A brief description of Orkney, Zetland, Pightland-Firth and Caithness,* published in 1701, wrote:

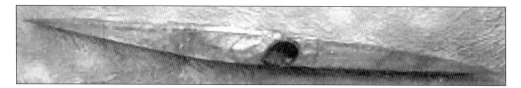

The Kayak.

'There are frequently *Finn-men* seen here upon the Coasts, as one about a year ago on *Stronsa*, and another within these few months on *Westra*, a Gentleman with many others in the Isle looking on him nigh to the shore, but when any endeavour to apprehend them, they flee away most swiftly; which is very strange that one man sitting in his little boat, should come some hundred of leagues, from their own Coasts as they reckon *Finland* to be from *Orkney*; it may be thought wonderful that they live all that time, and are able to keep the Sea so long. His boat is made of Seal skins, or some kind of leather, he also hath a coat of leather upon him, and he sitteth in the middle of his boat, with a little oar in his hand, fishing with his lines: And when in a storm he seeth the high surge of a wave approaching, he hath a way of sinking his boat, till the wave pass over, least thereby he should be overturned. The Fishers observe that these *Finmen* or *Finland-Men*, by their coming drive away the Fishes from the Coasts. One of their boats is kept as a Rarity in the *Physician's Hall at Edinburgh*.'

In addition to these accounts one might take into account two harpoon heads of Inuit type discovered at Collieston and Cullen on the Scottish coast, as well as a third one found at Tara in County Down Ireland, which suggest some level of Inuit presence in the North Sea at the turn of the eighteenth century. Proponents of such an idea point to the 'little ice age' around 1300 to 1850 when ice floes would have stretched further south than today and offer the Faeroe Islands, Shetland and Orkney as places to rest and collect water between Greenland and northern Scotland. Perhaps, however, all the openness of such questions explains is the volume of scholarly attention that this topic has attracted, particularly over the last century. For myself I am inclined to view these stories as an example of how stories, academic, journalistic and folklore, gather and develop around explanations of material objects, particularly those with the air of mystery and wonder at the sad story of a man who found himself far from home.

Anders Ingram

The excise officer

A dying breed now in Aberdeen is the Customs and Excise Officer. I served as one in the 1950s in bonded warehouses, mainly in the harbour area and particularly in Watson's bond(No. 7) and Gordon Graham's (No. 4). There I saw pretty closely how they ran.

There always seemed to be a happy atmosphere in the warehouses whether because of or despite the drink, with plenty of humour around. In No. 7, for example, I remember the occasion when we were bottling Glen Grant single malt whisky and some staff were in the C & E office toasting a wee, unofficial sampler. The carter (horse and cart in those days), one of the porters, noticed this and asked 'far wis his een'. I pointed to a sample tube containing about a standard half–bottle of blended whisky at five degrees proof and said 'try that for size'. A short while later the empty tube was banged down on the tray. I asked what had happened to the contents to be reminded I had said it 'wis his een'. The drink had no effect on the big man!

On another occasion one of my watchers, after a prolonged visit to a local hostelry, was found 'topping up' from a bottle of Federal Law export whisky from the bond.

From Graham's bond, which bottled both beer and whisky, my memories are slightly dimmer, not however with Black Bottle. The whisky in the 1950s was eight years old, substantially older than most of the blends at the time. This was because of a 'knock-on' effect caused by the suspension of distillation at distilleries during the Second World War. In fact in the same context I can remember

Virginia Street, where many bonded warehouses stood. (Aberdeen Art Gallery and Museums Collection)

refusing permission to Arthur Bell of Perth to pump a bottling into a glass-lined vat. This was because the whisky would not have qualified for its three years in oak certificate, a strict legal requirement.

While working in the bond there was a George Booth employed on the beer-bottling operation, while John Lobban was foreman on the whisky side. Bottling was in the region of two hundred and fifty cases per week with blending about every three months to cope with the level of bottling.

There was a memorable time when one of the bottling girls was suspected of taking the odd bottle out of the warehouse and I remember finding a full half bottle in one of the supposedly empty crates. It was decided that, rather than confront her on flimsy evidence, we'd substitute a similar bottle of water, coloured to the correct standard and properly sealed. We often wondered what her boyfriend though of that particular 'cairry

oot'. The same girl got her marching orders later when her knicker elastic snapped as she was passing the 'high heid yins' outside, a bottle dropping and smashing on the cassies. Customs and Excise work wasn't all serious.

The bottling sequence was simple – bottle 250 cases and remnant; count the bottles; cork them; affix labels; then pack the cases. There was an anomaly concerning the liquid quantity in the bottles. The measure for the bottles was 12 = 2 gallons, but the measure for half bottles (reputed pints) was 24 = 1. 998 gallons, so that two pints was less than one quart. To cover this half bottles were invoiced as two and a half gill flasks.

Occasional passing trade for the warehouse was in the form of trawlermen dying for a drink after a three week trip. They would try to barter with a 'fry' of lemon sole which I thought smelled as I was brought up eating only the best – line caught fish

Andy Duff

4 The Harbour at the Heart of the City

Harbour reflections

The Aberdeen Harbour I first came to know while a schoolboy in the early 1960s had an old-fashioned charm, which made it a source of constant interest. An Edwardian seafarer would have found much that was familiar, and even some of the veteran Aberdeen colliers bore a passing resemblance to the steam coasters of the early years of the twentieth century.

A casual study of then-and-now photographs of the harbour, especially the Upper Dock area, showed not a great deal had changed. There were the same quays along which railway tracks threaded their way round the harbour, and the same granite setts over which countless horse-drawn and motor lorries had rumbled. There were even the same transit sheds and, then as now, Aberdeen's city-centre skyline was dominated by the clock towers of the town house and the harbour office and the elegant spire of St Nicholas Kirk. This image of the past was sometimes completed by the sight of the Victorian steam industrial locomotive, slowly puffing along the harbour lines, drawing a rake of coal wagons and bound for the gasworks in Cotton Street. You could find a Sentinel steam wagon at work on Albert Quay, and even the occasional horse-drawn cart could be seen in the harbour area until the late 1960s.

The ships which inspired the most interest for me were the colliers owned by the local coal merchants. There were five colliers employed in the rough and dirty coal trade in 1963, and they ranged from the grand old *Thrift* of 1931 to the modern *Spray* of 1962, both of which were built by the Aberdeen shipyard of Hall Russell & Co, and reflected a time when ship owners showed admirable loyalty to their local shipbuilders. The *Thrift*'s usual discharging berth was at Upper Quay, which runs parallel with Market Street, right in the heart of the city. For Aberdonians who glanced in the direction of the *Thrift*, this elderly, coal-burning steam coaster was a visible symbol of Aberdeen's long and close connection with the sea. Many years later I spoke to Mr A. Leiper, who had been the *Thrift*'s chief engineer, about his time aboard the ship. He told me that the old ship used to blot her copybook while in port by raising steam before she sailed. A sizeable amount of coal was needed for this and resulting black smoke from her tall funnel used to swirl up Market Street, provoking the wrath of the Douglas Hotel's manager. The *Thrift* later had to burn smokeless fuel when in port, but when she sailed from Aberdeen for the last time in 1968, several shovel-fulls of coal sprinkled on to her furnace produced the required smoke needed by the TV camera crew recording her departure for the breakers' yard.

The scene at nearby Jamieson's Quay, where Ellis and McHardy's *Spray* discharged her coal, was possibly the nosiest and dirtiest at the harbour. Great clouds of coal dust shot up when a grab crane emptied coal into waiting lorries. Another crane would deposit coal into a hopper of a clattering coal-sifting machine. The coal was then filled into sacks, weighed and stacked up on the quayside by men begrimed with black dust.

There were other interesting ships which brought much cleaner cargoes, such as esparto grass and woodpulp, the essential raw materials for Aberdeen's papermaking industry. A wartime-built tramp steamer flying the Lebanese flag merited a mention in a local newspaper in the early 1960s, arriving from Algiers with esparto grass. About ten years earlier, the *Nicos*, under her earlier name of *Athenic*, had been a constant source of trouble to Aberdeen's harbourmaster, especially during gales, when she was laid up at one of the buoys in the Victoria Deck. On one occasion, when she broke her moorings, she collided with and slightly damaged a newly-built factory trawler.

Some years later the master of another tramp steamer, the *Vaigu*, used one of the old mooring buoys in the Victoria Dock to assist his departure from Blaikie's Quay, after discharging woodpulp from Finland. One of the Harbour Board's boatmen passed a hawser through the buoy's ring and the *Viagu* was warped round so that she faced the dock enterance. Once the manoeuvre was completed, a couple of turns of her propellor allowed her to pass through the upraised St Clement's Bridge and out onto the Navigation Channel. It was an excellent demonstration of ship-handling, which had been accomplished without modern aids such as bow-thrusters.

Steamships were not the most economic of ships to operate in the early 1970s and the *Viagu* was replaced on the woodpulp run by the motorship *Becky*. The *Becky* conjured up images of the Baltic and Scandinavia one winter's evening at Blaikie's Quay, as snowflakes swirled around her funnel, illuminated by floodlights to allow the uploading of her woodpulp cargo. Several dockers had their parka hoods drawn up tightly

The Thrift.

The Spray.

against their chins, and they stamped their frozen feet on the bales of woodpulp already stacked up on the snow-covered quayside. The red glow of a brazier offered some welcome warmth on the bitterly cold November night.

Other ships had made the long voyage to Aberdeen from warmer climes, bringing bulk cargoes such as phosphate from Morocco and Senegal, and pumice gravel from the Italian island of Lipari. Phosphate was in heavy demand for the manufacture of compound fertilisers at the Sandilands works near the beach. One old-timer, which brought several phosphate cargoes in 1972/73, was the bulk

The Vaigu – *a typical Baltic tramp.*

carrier *Yebala*, which had been converted to her new role from a former Shell oil tanker. Aberdeen-manufactured fertiliser was occasionally exported from the harbour as part of Britain's overseas aid programme, and found its way to countries as diverse as Kenya, Pakistan and the Philippines. The steam cargo liner *Ben Attow*, of the celebrated Ben Line of Leith, loaded 7,000 tons of fertiliser for the Philippines in early 1975. Her chief officer was a 'Torry loon' while her second fireman also came from Aberdeen, but from the place of that name in Hong Kong.

The north-east's house-building boom of the 1970s produced an insatiable demand for pumice gravel, which was used to make breeze blocks. One of the biggest single consignments from Lipari came on the Bulgarian bulk carrier *Persenk*, which brought 13,000 tons of pumice in May 1973. She had to swing anchor in the bay for a week before there was a sufficiently high tide to carry her over the bar at the entrance to the harbour. Five years later another bulk carrier, the *Nicolas Maris*, encountered a similar tidal

problem when she arrived from Lipari. The enforced delay resulted in food and water being taken out to her crew, who were running short of supplies. The harbour's pilots and tugboat crews had their skills tested to the limit when these large, unwieldy ships arrived at the port. However, their docking and undocking always seemed to be accomplished with consummate ease.

Aberdeen has had a long-standing trade with North America. In the 1960s, at the appropriately named Atlantic and Pacific Wharves, the cargo steamers of Ellerman's Wilson Line of Hull made an impressive sight while unloading flour from Canada. Their names such as *Bassano*, *Marengo* and *Rialto*, had a lovely resonance, matched by their colourful appearance of green hulls, white masts and upperworks, and a black-topped red funnel, which prompted their nickname of 'green parrots.'

Within a few years Aberdeen had emerged as the principal supply base for the oil and gas fields in the British sector of the nothern North Sea. The import of oil-related

Unloading timber in the heart of the city.

The St Clement Bridge is raised to allow access to Victoria Dock. The bridge was closed in 1974.

hardware from the US ports on the Gulf of Mexico saw a restoration of Aberdeen's trading links with North America in 1973. The Harrison Line of Liverpool maintained the service from Houston and New Orleans, and by the end of 1973, a Harrison Liner was to be seen in the port almost every fortnight. My father had served as a cadet

The Persenk, *at the limits of cargo capacity.*

The St Clair *at Mathew's Quay.*

with the Harrison Line between 1928-32 and took a special interest in their ships' arrivals. The visit of Harrison's *Scholar* in September 1973 stirred memories for him of a much earlier *Scholar*, which was a coal-burning cargo steamer, in which he had voyaged from Liverpool to the West Indies in 1930.

The sailing of an ocean-going cargo liner from Aberdeen was always an inspirational sight. The Harrison Line's *Philosopher* seemed almost within touching distance as she slipped past the Round House at Footdee in May 1973, and any person with a love of the sea would have wished to be aboard her. There always seemed a greater, more exciting world

The Philosopher *– a sign of the emerging oil industry.*

The Harrison Line's Explorer.

On board the Craiglynne, *the trawling industry was soon to face disastrous decline.*

Life on the trawlers was seldom easy.

Jim Murray, Craiglynne's *helmsman, keeps a close eye on the compass.*

waiting to be discovered beyond the North Pier. I did sail beyond the North Pier in several contrasting ships during the 1970s. HMS *Thornham*, a converted inshore minesweeper, was the Aberdeen University Royal Naval Unit's seagoing tender, on board which students endeavoured to put practice into their classroom instruction in seamanship and navigation. The *Thornham* was more suited to navigation in shallow waters such as estuaries and rivers, and she could be quite lively out in the North Sea as she headed for

ports such as Arbroath, Fraserburgh, Macduff and Peterhead. This well-travelled ship met a bizarre end in 1981 when a Harbour Board crane toppled on to her while she was berthed at Regent Quay. Nobody was hurt in the incident, but badly damaged *Thornham* was assessed as being only fit to be broken up.

It was from Aberdeen that you could make the longest sea voyage within the British Isles as a fare-paying passenger. In August 1973, I made a return trip to Lerwick on the 1960 built *St Clair*, the then flag ship of the North

Laid–up trawlers herald the decline of the industry.

of Scotland, Orkney and Shetland Shipping Co. She was an elegant ship, but had become a trifle old fashioned because her passenger facilities were sharply divided into first and second class, which was out of place in the era of one class roll on roll off ferries. Thick fog enveloped Aberdeen when the *St Clair* sailed, and the bell tolling at the end of the North Pier sounded quite eerie in the gloom. Her passengers included holiday makers, backpackers, commercial travellers and Shetlenders returning home.

On my next voyage to the Northern Isles, the only other passengers, apart from myself, were livestock destined for Kirkwall. The ship was the *St Rognvald*, a cargo and passenger ship, which had been built in Aberdeen in 1955 by Alexander Hall and Co, a celebrated builder of clipper ships for the China tea and Australian wool trades in the nineteenth century. Hall's had lost none of their touch and the *St Rognvald* was a lovely looking ship with a graceful sheer. Soon after my trip aboard her in 1978 she was replaced on the Northern Isles' run by the inevitable roll on-roll off ferry.

A year later, the next trip beyond the North Pier was made on another Aberdeen built vessel, but one which offered considerably less comfort than the *St Rognvald*. The Aberdeen scratcher trawler *Craiglynn* had been built in 1960 by the John Lewis yard in Torry which in the previous year had launched no fewer than eleven trawlers, most of them destined for Aberdeen owners. The *Craiglynn* shot her first trawl thirty-five miles south-east of Aberdeen, but the three and a half-day trip yielded a disappointing catch, despite the excellent spring weather. My trip on the *Craiglynn* had given me a vivid, first-hand, experience of North-Sea trawling, tempered by the fact that I was witnessing the dramatic decline of Aberdeen's trawling industry. Only a few years later the *Craiglynn*'s owners were forced into receivership as a direct result of soaring operating costs, and poor quayside prices for fish.

At the start of the 1970s I was glad I had seen something of the last flourish of the Aberdeen trawler fleet. One of the more picturesque sites to be seen from the beach esplanade was the trawlers putting to sea on a

Monday morning in the summertime. Their masts could be followed filing past the North Pier. As they emerged out into the bay, the knowledgable could identify the ownership of a trawler by her hull and funnel colours. Upon reaching the open water, the trawlers fanned out and headed for the fishing grounds, some for the Faroes, others for Shetland and the west-side grounds, while the scratchers set course for the east course grounds. All hoping for a good haul from Aberdeen Bank, the Buchan Deeps, the Stirling Bank or the Turbot Bank.

I had glimpsed the harvest of the sea being landed at Aberdeen fish market on a couple of occasions, and had been impressed by the huge size of the skate and the iniqitous look of the dogfish.

The nearby fish-market café on Commercial Quay was a welcome refuge, not only for fish-market workers, but also for early morning travellers who had arrived by train at Aberdeen, and wanted to kill time before catching the first bus home. There was a cruel frost on the December morning I visited it. The fish-market porters trooped into the café for a soul restoring bowl of porridge and a mug of tea, and as they bantered with one another they looked almost as frozen as the fish they had hoisted out of the trawler's holds. Aberdeen harbour has seen many economic vicissitudes over the past 800 years, but has always successfully adapted to the prevailing trends in trade. The port may be a busier and more profitable place than when I first became acquainted with it forty years ago, but I still yearn for those days when ships looked like ships, had character and history.

Peter Myers

Navigating the channel

On the south side of the entrance to Aberdeen harbour, marking the inner end of the channel, there is a small breakwater projecting northwards, and like a thumb on a right hand a small mole sprouts from the shoreward end of this breakwater. This curious extremity is topped by a capstan, now rusty and leaning but once an essential part of the harbour navigation system.

A visit to the capstan reveals nothing about it, other than the fact that amazingly, it still turns. So those who are curious about its use have to delve into the history of the port, starting with the old maps of the harbour.

Probably the most famous of the maps is that drawn by Peter May in 1756. He was a surveyor employed by the magistrates of Aberdeen to produce an accurate map of the port, because they mistrusted the previous work. This map shows a large river estuary with islands in the stream, and a cluster of houses on the north shore which was the city. The estuary narrows into something looking not unlike the channel of today apart from the fact that there is no stonework. The course of the river Dee is to the north and then curving back southward towards the entrance.

On the south side of the approach to the port there are a number of sticks which might be positioned to guide vessels, and alarmingly the sea outside the port is known on the plan as the German Ocean. There is no sign of any moles or breakwaters, let alone capstans. Hence one can assume that back in 1756 the sailing vessels wishing to enter the harbour either waited for the best wind to allow them to sail up the channel, or else were towed up the estuary by rowing boats. In Glasgow at the same time sailing ships were towed up to Port Glasgow by teams of horses but this option was not open to the seafarers entering Aberdeen because the coast was rocky.

In order to ease this passage and to protect the harbour, breakwaters were constructed over the next fifty years. The harbour as we know it today began to be developed and the river Dee was re-routed to the south into the

The harbour has been a constantly changing feature of the city's past and present.

channel in which it now flows. But the single most important event for those who were challenged at every arrival by the difficulties of negotiating the entrance to the Dee, was the launching of the *Paul Jones*, at Halls shipyard on 22 August 1827. The *Paul Jones* was Aberdeen's first steam tug. The first tug on the Clyde had entered service in 1819, so the new technology had taken some time to reach the Northeast.

A local history states that the tug 'replaced the labourers on the piers who had previously hauled vessels into the port entrance using capstans', and there seems to be no other evidence of the purpose of the capstans, or indeed that they were ever used. But even this scant reference allows us to assume that during the construction of the port prior to the beginning of the nineteenth century, someone realised that it might be more efficient to haul the ships in, rather than to row them in.

Probably the same rowing boats were used to take long lines from the ships and ferry them to the north side and the south side of the harbour, where waiting labourers would take several turns round the barrels of the capstans. A couple of labourers would keep hold of the ends of the ropes and at least half a dozen would push the capstans round with long staves located in the slots on the top. Once in the harbour the ships could then sail on across what is now the tidal basin into the Victoria Dock area where they could either drop anchor or warp their way inward to the berths.

A further 900 feet was added to the pier in 1812, and a final 500 foot section was added in 1870. Both are of noticeably different construction from the original. On the south side breakwaters pointing north were added at approximately the same easterly longitude as the end of the pier, the final 'new' south breakwater giving a certain majesty to the entrance.

These additions to the length of the pier may have been due in part to the continuing failure of merchant ships to successfully navigate the channel. In 1804, when the pier was very short, the sailing coaster the *Hawk*, was driven onto the beach just to the north of it. Subsequent to the construction of the 1812 extension, spectators would gather at the seaward end when easterly gales were blowing just to watch the fun. Even today it is difficult to bring a ship up the channel in strong easterlies and the port is closed when the harbourmaster feels there is a chance of the ships bottoming in the channel. In the early part of the nineteenth century sailing ships would gamely make for the entrance knowing that, whatever the risk, they faced the possibility of being blown ashore in any case. Even if they managed to get into the channel they could be picked up on the swell and dashed into the south breakwater, or onto the ledge which still protrudes beneath the water inside the North Pier.

There were many wrecks, and often the spectators on the pier were able to assist with the rescue of the passengers and crew of the stricken vessels. Even though the tug was available after 1827 ship-owners were as conservative as they are now, and were reluctant to arrange for a tow when it seemed likely that their vessels could get in on their own. Since it took several hours to get up steam the *Paul Jones* was virtually useless as a lifeboat and the crew could only watch helplessly as the wrecks took place.

In 1839 the paddle steamer *Brilliant* was caught by a swell and piled up on the end of the North Pier, which sloped into the sea. The spectators helped the passengers and crew ashore in the usual manner, but no-one remembered to put the fires out. As a result when the water in the boiler dried up the vessel blew up in a spectacular fashion.

A key to the past.

An oil-supply vessel provides a contrast between the old and the new at the harbour entrance.

This was the first steam ship to be wrecked in the port and may have suggested to the harbour authorities that even steamers were not immune to the dangers of the harbour entrance, so it may not be chance that the leading lights were completed in 1843. Two further tugs, the *Dorothy* and the *Samson* entered service in the same year, doubtless allowing larger ships to enter, since they would no longer be dependent on the ropes, the labourers and the capstans. For these larger vessels to avoid the dangers of the North Pier and the South Breakwater they would need to keep to the deepest part of the channel, and therefore they would have a greater need for direction.

The same leading lights are still in service today, although now powered by electricity rather than oil, and the port has continued to develop although there has been no building on the south side beyond what is now the entrance to the river Dee. This is because of the possibility of scouring of the river bed and because it is claimed by some that the original North breakwater was not in fact built in exactly the right direction. As a result the Tidal Basin remains exposed to easterly winds, and the small mole with its derelict capstan remains as the sole reminder of the difficulties the old sailing ship masters had when they were entering the port of Aberdeen.

Vic Gibson

The Torry battery – a neglected treasure.

I was one of over a hundred people gathered at the Torry battery at dusk on 3 June 2002 to observe the culmination of Aberdeen's diamond jubilee celebrations. The crowd

The Torry battery. (Aberdeen Central Library).

cheered as ninety-one-year-old Ted Munro, known locally as Mr Torry, lit the twelve foot beacon to commemorate the Queen's fifty year reign. The fire took hold and the flames began to flicker and snake upwards into the sky. As I watched the torch burn furiously, my gaze was diverted to the bleak, crumbling structure chosen as the venue for this prestigious event.

Although I had been a frequent visitor to the Torry battery over the years, it had never occurred to me to investigate the history behind this historic site. As far back as I can remember the battery had been an ideal sheltered spot for a family picnic, not to mention a favourite haunt for courting couples.

Surrounded by the Balnagask golf course and dwarfed by the Girdleness lighthouse, the battery ruins offer an excellent panoramic view of the harbour. Beyond are the impressive towers of the modern city, with the ancient spires of Old Aberdeen in the distance. However what's left of the battery is less impressive. The once imposing coastal defence

site has been become a hollow, neglected shell. The outer walls remain virtually intact and offer shelter from the bitter cold winds sweeping in from the North Sea. Inside, only a crumbling ruin situated to the left of the gate remains of the fortress infrastructure. These had been the guardhouse, store and flank emplacements. The other buildings had been demolished during the 1950s.

It struck me that, although I had lived in Torry for over forty years, I had very little knowledge of the battery. I knew it was built to defend our coastline from enemy ships, but beyond that my knowledge was negligible. When was it built? Why was it built? Who used it? When did it fall into disuse? What's its story? There's nothing immediately obvious up there to tell you. When my companion informed me it had been inhabited as recently as the early fifties my enthusiasm was fired up, and I had to find out more.

There have actually been two forts on this site. The first can be traced back to the outbreak of the French revolution. In 1794 Arthur Gibbon formed the Aberdeen Battery

Company to protect the city and the harbour entrance from enemy ships. However the original fort was allowed to fall into disrepair and it wasn't until half a decade had passed that work began on the second battery.

Building work commenced on the new fort in 1857 and was designed by R.R. Anderson R.E. By the time work was completed in 1860 the project had cost £7,236. The Torry battery was built with the main armaments facing north-east. An ornate gate was built to the south-west. The officer's mess, store, battery offices and barrack rooms were housed to the right of the main entrance with a narrow parade ground in the centre. The fort had two caponiers - projections from the wall that provide flanking fire. The open caponier faced towards the sea while the covered caponier, or bastion, flanked the main gate.

The battery was operated by members of the City of Aberdeen Volunteer Rifle Corps and accommodated approximately ninety men. The fortress was fully equipped with weapons to prevent unauthorised ships from entering the harbour. The armaments in 1865 consisted of seven 64-pounders and were armed by placing the shell into the muzzle. Another muzzle loading gun was added in 1880. And during the First World War a couple of 6-inch breech-loading weapons were added. These guns were similar in style to the others except that the shells were loaded from the rear.

The weapons were never fired at enemy ships but there is a record of them being used to try to help recover the body of a local businessman. Local shipyard owner Walter Hood was drowned in 1862 after slipping in the dark and falling into the harbour. The battery guns were fired in the hope that the concussion would bring the body to the surface but grappling irons were needed to recover the corpse.

On the 8 June 1905 a strip of land along Baxter Street and Victoria Road was sold to the commissioners for the Lord High Admiral for the United Kingdom. This was to allow the road approaching the battery to be widened, giving troops easier access to Torry Point. This move was prompted by the start of the Russian revolution.

The battery wasn't staffed on a permanent basis until the First World War in 1914. The site was fully manned twenty-four hours a day throughout the duration of the war. The guns remained in position between the wars but the battery wasn't fully staffed again until the outbreak of the Second World War. At this point considerable improvements were made to protect the installation from air attacks. Searchlights and anti-aircraft guns were installed to offer more protection during air raids. Two royal navy guns were placed at Girdleness and three Howitzers were installed at the battery. During both wars the gunners came from Wallasey in Cheshire.

There were five fatalities during an air raid in 1941. Four soldiers from the Royal Artillery, and one member of the Royal Engineers, were killed when two bombs were dropped on the battery. The big guns were eventually fired later that year. Two unidentified vessels were seen approaching the harbour on the 3 June 1941. The order was given to fire at them and then swiftly countermanded when it was established that these ships were British. The vessels had failed to give the correct signals when approaching the port. A month later the machine guns were fired at an enemy plane that had dropped bombs off Kinnaird Head. The plane was eventually shot down at St Cyrus.

During each of the wars the roads leading to the battery were blocked off and only military staff were allowed access to Torry Point. The regular army finally vacated the battery when the war finished in 1945. The territorials took over the manning of the battery but had to share with 'squatters.' Aberdeen had been heavily bombed during the war and this created a severe housing shortage. Many families were either homeless, or living in overcrowded conditions. Between 1945 and 1952 the battery was used to alleviate the problem while the house-building programme was undertaken. The buildings provided accommodation for seven families

The battery guns were briefly re-activated during the 1956 Suez crisis prior to full decommissioning in 1957. The site was sold within months to the local council, who have retained ownership since then. It was turned into a public park and picnic area during the 1960s.

The battery was the ideal focal point to view a magnificent spectacle during the last decade. Thousands of people lined up alongside the ruins when Aberdeen hosted the tall ships race. The magnificent sailing vessels sailed past the fort twice, once in 1991 and again in 1997. On these occasions the battery played host to two temporary radio stations set up to cover the event for spectators.

Recently another landmark was added to the Torry Point skyline. The Torry Heritage Society erected a monument to seafarers who lost their lives at sea. Situated beside the battery car park the monument took the form of a granite cairn depicting rolling waves, surmounted by a stainless steel cross. A granite slab with a suitable inscription is incorporated into the base of the cairn. The Lord Provost of Aberdeen performed the unveiling on 12 September 2001. The Heritage Society has recently launched a fundraising scheme to light up the monument.

And that is the history of the Torry battery – as far as I know. I've no doubt there are many more tales to tell it's just that I haven't been able to find any. What surprised me is how little is known about the fort. Although the second battery had a lifespan of nearly a century, and despite the fact that it had successfully defended Aberdeen harbour

through two world wars and numerous overseas skirmishes only a scant amount of information remains. It seems that our ancestors had neglected the battery as much as we have. They didn't think it worthy enough to keep detailed records.

For over forty years the vast majority of Aberdonians have ignored the ruins of this once important building. Next time you're driving past, or playing a round of golf at Balnagask, stop for a moment and take a look. Walk around the old place and absorb the marvellous sense of history it imbues. I promise that you won't regret it.

Gordon Bathgate

Aberdeen Sailors' Home

Out of sight maybe but certainly not out of mind as far as I am concerned. It is more than twenty years now since Aberdeen Sailors' Home ceased to be a 'home' for seafarers. The British Sailors' Society Sailors' Home in Mearns Street has been in existence since 1868, when the original building was erected with funds raised by public subscription. After reconstruction work in 1944 the main part of the present building was officially opened by the then Princess Elizabeth. A further extension was opened in 1965 by Her Majesty the Queen Mother, and this is where my story begins.

I was appointed manager of the home on the 5 August 1964 , and left in the summer of 1974 to study for the ministry in the Church of Scotland. During those ten years the Sailors' Home was a hive of activity with accommodation – after the extension was opened – for sixty-four seafarers. I employed eighteen staff to help run the Sailors' Home which was open twenty-four hours a day. These included kitchen staff, waitresses, cleaners, porters, canteen lady, handyman and a receptionist. Dock labourers, staff at Shore

Veteran seafarer's Christmas party.

Porter's Society and workers at Hamlyn's grain store all took advantage of the restaurant and canteen facilities available. We served on average 200 meals a day, including breakfast, dinner and tea. I lived on the premises in a flat at the back of the home overlooking James Street, with my wife and three children.

The British Sailors' Society, being a charitable organization, employed a full-time port missionary whose job was to visit all merchant ships entering the port, mainly to check on the ship's library which was provided by the society, and to change the books if necessary. Also he would visit the homes of retired veteran seafarers or widows with offers of financial support where needed, visit the hospitals to enquire if any seafarers had been admitted, hold regular Sunday evening worship in the Mariner's Chapel at the rear of the Sailors' Home and, most difficult of all, convey tragic news to seafarers families of death or accident at sea. Being a port missionary myself for four years, both in Leith and Methil, we worked together as colleagues for days off and holiday relief.

With the tremendous development of the Port of Aberdeen, because of North Sea Oil activities, the home became increasingly important to many seamen who found it a real home-from-home. It also provided residential accommodation and meals for maritime students, while studying for various seagoing certificates. On Christmas Day there was a free Christmas dinner for all seafarers, as was the custom of the society in its hostels. Over and above that I organised a free Christmas dinner – usually during the first week in the new year – for all veteran seafarers in the port, with the help and liaison of the Seaman's Union and the Mercantile Marine Office.

When Her Majesty the Queen Mother visited the home on 13 May 1965 to open the

Student mariners being presented to the Queen Mother.

extension, Lord Provost Norman Hogg was waiting to greet her when she alighted from the royal car. Mr H.J. Edwards, the honorary secretary of the society for over thirty-seven years, recalled with pleasure the opening of the Sailor's Home almost twenty-one years ago when the Queen, then Princess Elizabeth performed the official function. He told the assembly of the great benefit now for seafarers as the new extension now made it possible to accommodate twice as many mariners as before. Over 4,000 had slept in the home in the three months since its completion and over 12,000 had eaten there during that time. Before unveiling a commemorative plaque in the packed lounge, Her Majesty spoke of the great pleasure she experienced at being present as yet another milestone in the home's history was passed. I had the honour to escort Her Majesty on a tour of the building, including a visit to the chapel where the port missionary, veteran seafarers and their wives,

and my own family saw her. Seven months after her visit the Queen Mother sent four large boxes of chocolates from Clarence House to be distributed as a Christmas treat for the veterans seafarer's annual dinner.

When I left in the summer of 1974 the Sailors' Home was still thriving. After a few years numbers started to decline owing to the downturn of merchant shipping. The British Sailors' Society during my fifteen years in their employment was unique in that it had a mission to seafarers in most Scottish ports and had its headquarters in Clyde Street, Glasgow. Now I believe it is known as the British & International Sailors' Society – this says it all.

The dock area and the buildings in and around Mearns Street are all used for different purposes compared to the 1960s. For me and my wife, my two daughters and son this was an era, now past, but with many happy memories which shall never be forgotten.

William Watt

5 Wartime

A youngster's view
Prize Winning Entry

My first job after leaving school was as an office boy with a shipping office down at the quay. My family had connections with the quay and boats for many years, and my desire was to go to sea as a cadet on reaching sixteen years old. This first job at least gave me a taste of what boats were all about. Within days of war being declared the whole dock area was sealed off with fencing and barbed wire for reasons for security. This meant a pass was required for access. To a young lad there was plenty of excitement, meeting with the captains of various ships, and one of my first jobs was to meet ships for which we acted on arrival at the dock gates. On boarding I located the master and had to make out passes for all the crew - a big deal for a youngster.

My duties were varied, and each day brought a new challenge. Before arriving at the office I had to cycle from my home in Mannofield to the North Pier office at

The Marischal Street bomb.

Bombs fell throughout the city – as here at Great Northern Road.

Stafford Street was hit during the raid.

Hilton Terrace – residential rubble.

Footdee, and list all the arrivals and sailings for the previous day. I then proceeded to the office where my boss, one John G. Gill was the local rep for the Ministry of Shipping. This information was then typed and sent to the masters of ships for whom we were the agents. They had to report to the naval base (The Station Hotel) to get their sailing instructions for when a convoy was due off Aberdeen.

The port of Aberdeen was a key port in the supply of goods being shipped to Scapa Flow. Cargo boats such as the *Cantick Head, St Abbs Head* or *Denwick Head* sailed regularly between Aberdeen and Lyness, Orkney with thousands of tons of cement for the Churchill barriers. Other goods were also shipped on a regular weekly run.

Shipbuilding continued during the war and we had three main companies- Hall Russell,

Alex Hall & Son and John Lewis - all with an excellent reputation. Hall Russell and John Lewis mostly built cargo vessels while A. Hall & Son specialised in tugs. Our company acted for many of these new ships, and it was always with great interest we saw them completed and ready to sail to ports throughout the world.

Locally-owned colliers were well known by all at the quay. They carried coal from ports in the North of England, Seaham, Blyth, Sunderland, North Shields and Methil in Fife. Each had the experience of being attacked by German bombers many times, as the bombers made their way across the North Sea.

The harbour area was always a target for the German bombers and I well remember arriving at the office and passing a huge crater at the bottom of Marischal Street. This caused havoc for many days. I also recall vividly the day Hall Russell got a direct hit, which caused many casualties. The Bomber however was chased by Spitfires from Dyce and finally crashed into the ice rink in South Anderson Drive. The ice rink was in the process of being built and that finished that project. For many years the tyre marks could be seen where the aircraft hit the road before its final plunge.

I was a member of the 44th Boy's Brigade attached to Mannofield church, Aberdeen. Each year the Boy's Brigade held what was called 'The Demonstration' in the Music Hall, Aberdeen. It comprised the best of the Boy's Brigade activities and each company had an opportunity to complete and enter a team. Members of each company were invited to attend, and hopefully learn from what they saw at the 'Demonstration'. The said demonstration for 1943 was to be held on 21 April, commencing at 7. 30 p.m.

With some fellow members of the 44th company we made our way to the music hall that night and it was most instructive to see other lads our age on the horse, the bars, marching and many other events. We as onlookers were very envious that we did not have the skills that these lads had. All went well and we emerged from the music hall around 10 p.m., crossing Union Street to catch the No. 2 Mannofield tramcar home. Yes, in those days trams were the mode of transport, and each route had its own coloured

Kittybrewster rail-sheds damaged.

The infamous ice-rink crash.

light to indicate in black out condition which tram was approaching. The No. 2 was green, the Dee to Don was No. 1 and red, Hazlehead was purple, and so on.

We duly boarded the tram, but only got as far as the junction of Great Western Road and Holburn Street when we were asked to leave the tram as the air-raid siren had sounded. Nothing unusual about that, and we decided to walk the rest of the journey home. However that was not to be. We had just walked a few yards when we heard the enemy planes coming in low and the three of us took shelter at Archibalds the House Furnishers. The drone of the aircraft got nearer and nearer and the next we knew there was an almighty explosion. This was a bomb that had made a direct hit on a tenement property in Ashvale Place (around 200 yards from where we were). A piece of shrapnel hit the wall opposite and

rebounded towards our shelter hitting me on the thigh. Within a matter of minutes the planes came over again and more bombs were released throughout the city. By this time neighbours from the adjoining property had taken to the basement, where the whole household were taking shelter.

At that time the McClymont Hall in Holburn Street was an A.R.P. station and being the nearest location, I was put on a stretcher and moved towards the hall. However at the Holburn Bar the bombers came over again and, to my amazement, I was lowered to the pavement while my stretcher bearers took shelter in a hallway. This was scary to say the least. However I duly arrived at the hall around midnight where a decision was made as to my injury. Doctors looked at it and decided surgery was needed. I was then taken to Woodend Hospital. In time I was

Menzies Road experiences the terror of bombing.

seen by a Mr Mair, the surgeon, and I was on the operating table by 2 a.m. My gash was sorted out and I was moved to a ward within the annexe, which housed soldiers who had been injured and sent home to Aberdeen.

I was to spend fourteen days in the annexe and grew up a lot during that time. Being a ward which housed soldiers, the Salvation Army came around each day with cigarettes and other items. While I was under age for a puff – only fifteen and a few months – I also enjoyed Woodbine cigarettes courtesy of the Salvation Army. While like other lads I had puffed a cigarette before this, this was to me finally maturing! It took twelve years before I would give up the weed for ever. Life in the annexe was interesting and time passed very quickly; a daily visit from the surgeon, Mr Mair monitored my injury and on the fourteenth day I was discharged home. Not

before the matron and her black labrador had bid me farewell at the main door.

On that terrible night in Aberdeen twenty-five Dornier Bombers dropped thirty-one tons of Bombs leaving ninety-seven people killed and 235 injured.

After six years at the harbour I finally got my wish and went to sea, not as a cadet but as an ordinary seaman on a coaste;, however that is another story.

Happy days they were, and it seems just like yesterday.

Derek Fraser

Growing up in wartime

'LOOK', said the man, 'Look over there on the horizon. Those ships are part of the fleet.' And he could point out the *Rodney, Nelson,*

Renown and *Royal Oak,* all romantic names which I knew, but never thought I would actually *see*. But there they were, sailing past mysteriously and majestically as we watched from the top deck of the *St Rognvald.*

We were on our way from Lerwick to Aberdeen, sailing indirect, and had just left Kirkwall harbour. It was 2 September 1939 and I had celebrated my ninth birthday the previous day. We arrived home in time to hear Mr Chamberlain's broadcast in which he told us that a state of war existed between Great Britain and Germany. Just a few hours later we heard the SS *Athena* had been sunk off the Hebrides. We were all shocked at the callous sinking of a passenger ship so soon after the outbreak of war.

We quickly got into the routine of wartime practices, such as blackout, when not a chink of light must be seen, and carrying our gas masks at all times. At school we had to put them on and rush down to the basement when the bell rang intermittently, signalling an air-raid practise, or perhaps the real thing.

There was a German girl called Helen Schweitzer who joined our class for three weeks en route to the United States with her family. Our teacher pounced on her at once and ranted and raved at her at every opportunity, so that she ran thankfully to her father, waiting each afternoon, at the gate. This astonishing display of blind prejudice stuck in my mind so that, although I knew Helen so briefly, I have never forgotten her, and hope that she found happiness in America after the rough time she had at our school.

There were ten of us in the household at the outbreak of war – my mother, Auntie Ruby, my brothers, sister and myself. Albert was the first to go to war, volunteering for service in the Royal Air Force. Hamish, Stanley and Harold got deferment until they finished university. Hugh, being employed at

Life went on, as it did here in Seaforth Road.

Hall Russell Shipyard, was in a reserved occupation.

Although far from the industrial belt, Aberdeen sustained more aerial attacks than any other Scottish city. For a long time, scarcely a night passed that we didn't hear the wail of the siren. We would all gather in the passageway downstairs, as faraway from the windows as possible, and listen for the wavering sound of the German planes, which was quite distinct from the steady drone of British ones. Every time the siren went Hugh had to run to the music hall, which served as a casualty centre. Hugh was in the ARP (Air Raid Precautions) and had to stand by to render first aid.

Two air raids stand out in memory. The first was at lunch time on a fine summer day in 1940, when a solitary Heinkel bombed Hall Russell's with considerable loss of life. Hugh was fortunate in having decided that day to take his lunch out along the beach to enjoy the sunshine. However, retribution was swift as pursuing Spitfires shot down the Heinkel which crashed into Aberdeen's new ice rink in South Anderson Drive. I got a small piece of wing as a souvenir.

The worst raid of all occurred in the spring of 1943 when extensive damage and loss of life was caused in various areas of the city. We experienced our nearest miss when a bomb fell in the next street demolishing about half of Carden Place Episcopal church. Our cousin, Fred, who lived in that street, just about opposite the church, was out in his garden watching the 'fun'. He being a First World War veteran was pretty blasé about it all, but I reckon that bomb was a bit close for comfort, even for him!

Food of course was rationed, but fish was not and, in Aberdeen, there was usually a fairly good supply. It usually seemed to be John who was sent to the fishmonger to pick up our order. One day as he came into the shop, he heard one of the assistants in the inner room discussing some kind of fish that nobody seemed to want. Then one of them had a brainwave, 'Give it to yon Shetland fowk' she said, 'they'll eat anything.' It offended John's sensitive nature, but how we did laugh when he told us, and it has been a family joke ever since.

When I think back to what we ate in wartime, the first thing that springs to mind is sheeps' heads, which probably bears out what the fish-shop assistant said! There was a plentiful supply of them in autumn and we ate them almost daily, since they would not have used up our precious coupons. I loved the tender and succulent tongue, cheeks and brains, but I drew the line at eating eyeballs! Harold ate them though, and took great delight in doing so in front of me. Of course a sheep's head also made a fine pot of broth.

It is interesting that even during the war there was always time for the personal touch. We had a very obliging grocer who mixed our butter and margarine rations together, thus producing a nice big piece of rather marbled 'butter'. As much as possible of our sugar ration was saved to make jams and jellies. We discovered a large group of bramble bushes growing near the edge of Rubislaw Quarry, Aberdeen's famous source of granite. My mother and her friend, Mrs Sutherland, and I spent many an afternoon there, taking a picnic tea with us. Brambles, when ripe, are big, black and inaccessible, guarded by the sharpest thorns, but we persevered in spite of the scratches and brought home pail-fulls of juicy berries with a light covering of granite dust. Auntie Ruby was the chief jam maker and soon we had rows of various preserves for the winter. I remember her once making rowanberry jelly from the small tree in our garden and it was a lovely brick-red colour and not nearly as sweet as other jams.

We had a map of Europe pinned up on the kitchen wall with small national flags that could be stuck in to chart the progress of the

Clearing up the wreckage.

war. During the dark days of 1940-41, there were far too many swastikas to be seen, but as the tide of war slowly turned, it was much more cheering to see Union Jacks and the flags of our allies dominating the scene.

We were all encouraged to 'dig for victory', and so most people dug up their flower beds and grew vegetables instead. Also plots of land were available on the outskirts of the town. We had one at Kaimhill and it was usually Hugh and Harold who tended it. They planted tatties and a few other vegetables and looked after them all through summer, but the biggest problem was getting the produce home. The plot was at least a mile and a half from home and the only transport they had was bicycles and an old motorbike, which might or might not be in running order. Also petrol was rationed and often that had been

used up. I think one time at least, they wheeled the motorbike over, piled as many sacks on it as possible and pushed it rather shakily back. They acquired another allotment later on, so it really kept my brothers busy.

At school it was decided that we could attend from 9 a.m. until 2 p.m. taking a light lunch with us, and then we were sent home with piles of homework to do. This measure was in order to save fuel, but I can't see that they saved much because they used so little anyway. In winter we were frozen stiff and were made to jump up and down in the hall after prayers, to get our circulation going before we went to our classrooms. One good thing they did was to plough up the hockey field just in time to prevent me from having to play the murderous game. I much preferred playing netball and tennis on the courts at the back of the school.

Hamish, Stanley and Harold had to do duty with the Home Guard. As well as the usual drill, target practice, route marches and parades, they had to turn out for all-night guard duty at places such as the gas works, bridges and the power station. Harold also got a holiday job digging air-raid shelters, which was back-breaking work, with a pick and shovel. Hamish and Harold went into the RAMC (Royal Army Medical Corps) and Stanley joined the Royal Air Force. John went straight from school into the army, starting off at the Gordon Barracks at the Bridge of Don. One day we heard an appeal on the radio for girls with Highers in scientific subjects to do war work. Violet fitted the bill, so off she went to what turned out to be laboratory work with the British Aluminium Company in the tiny village of Kinlochleven in the west of Scotland. I went to stay with her one summer and it took ten hours to get there by train. One evening she took me to a secret rendezvous in the hills where she bought me a coat on the 'black market'. Coupons were needed for clothing, but sometimes there were ways and means of acquiring a little extra.

Everyone was expected to do their bit for the war effort, so some of my friends and I borrowed a hand cart and went around the houses collecting waste paper. The cart filled up readily and we hauled it down to the depot in Little Chapel Street and received a few pennies for our efforts. I went with my mother to the Women's Guild and helped to clean sphagnum moss for use in dressings, instead of cotton wool, which was in very short supply. We also sewed old sheets and blankets together to make quilts.

Going to the pictures was the most popular pastime of the war years, and Aberdeen sported no less than fourteen cinemas. Some of us went two or three times a week and I had been in nearly every cinema in town – but not the Casino down near the beach. Rumour had it that that the entry fee was two empty jam jars, but that you were liable to leave with more than you went in with!

For us youngsters the beach was out of bounds and we couldn't go to the parks either, in case we were caught in an air-raid, so we played in the street and made full use of the double summer time which had been decreed. We played rounders, hopscotch and various complicated skipping and ball games, scattering for the very occasional car which appeared.

Our house was an ever-open half-way house to Shetlanders and others going to and from their work. There was always someone coming in along, or spending the night , or perhaps a short leave if they didn't have time to go home. But the time we always remember is the evening that six land-girls arrived from Shetland, needing a bed for the night. Somehow my mother got them all stowed away and they continued their journey in the morning.

Olive Walterson

6 The Past in the Present

Aberdeen: my journey

I have lived in the Aberdeen area for nineteen years, moving here with my parents when I was three. I have lived through many changes in the surroundings, and although I cannot possibly remember them all, there are some experiences I will never forget.

Camera in hand, I walked round my favourite areas of Aberdeen. I started off with the construction of the new Exhibition Centre. I feel this will be a more welcoming site to the north of the city. I remember when the old building was first erected; I used to call it the 'Crystal Castle'. In recent years it was definitely looking a bit worn and untidy. From here I walked along to the Bridge Of Don and the recently refurbished high-rise flats. The new-look structure stands out against the others and has a more practical sloping roof. Although many people do not like these tall, bland blocks I think they add something to the skyline. I must admit that I have never been inside one, but what a wonderful view there must be from the very top.

I decided to turn left at this point and journey onto the beach. The tide was on its way out and I was expecting to see a bustle of people on the sand, similar to the picture I had seen of the beach in the earlier part of the century. I knew of course there would be far fewer people, but was still quite shocked to see how few there were, after all it was mid-July. Families seemed to have whole sections of the beach to themselves, with the majority of

Multi-storey face lift.

Fittie remains as a reminder of past days in the city.

The Mercat Cross and Salvation Army Citadel.

The Town House.

activity taking place on the promenade, where people where cycling, roller-blading or just taking a leisurely stroll. The Aberdonians of today are not unique in preferring to head for the airport rather than the beach. Their grandparents may have done the same given the opportunity.

There has been a fantastic project to brighten up the area with some nautically inspired artwork. This mural has been done beautifully and adds life to this section of the beach. Unfortunately, vandals have been adding some artwork of their own to some of the figures, and have removed limbs here and there.

I carried on towards the small community of Footdee, known to locals as 'Fittie'. I have fallen in love with the small fishing village where a number of the old fishing bothies have been restored and put to new use. I like the miss-match of old forgotten bothies to the practical sheds and well-maintained miniature museums, full of trinkets and knick-knacks relating to the sea.

Shiprow has dramatically changed, even in recent years. The Maritime Museum's new location helped this area a lot. The road sweeps round from the old frontage of Doctor Drakes to the Trinity Congregational church that now houses the maritime museum. The museum itself turns one's thoughts to the sea with the sparkling blue glass that has also been used in the church's windows. The new section fits in beautifully between here and Provost Ross' house. A fantastic array of old and new that works excellently together.

The east end of Union Street has some magnificent architecture, including the Mercat Cross that stands in the centre of the Castlegate itself. The Town House is beautiful

Aberdeen Beach, a tranquil scene today.

Murals take the place of yesterday's crowds.

St Nicholas' House serves as a backdrop to Provost Skene's House.

Belmont Street from the rear.

Union Terrace Gardens.

Union Bridge shops, including Ottakar's.

Shiprow today.

from all angles; even the extension cannot be classed as ugly.

Today Provost Skene's house is a favoured building of Aberdonians, after being the survivor of a slum-clearance programme, and opened as a museum in 1953. The building was saved after a long-running campaign to stop its demolition, and is now blocked in by a high-rise office block and an unsightly car park. When the house was saved however it did not look so resplendent as it does today, and there was much restoration work to be carried out. Many great buildings were dismissed as slums and done away with in the history of Aberdeen, but you cannot entirely blame the people of the past for demolishing buildings that were in poor state of repair when starting afresh was the easiest thing to do.

The 1960s were a particularly disastrous time of renewal, when some of the ugliest building work was carried out throughout the country, and Aberdeen did not escape. However I do not think that all of the buildings erected during this era should be completely banished, as they themselves may become museum pieces in their own right.

I spent much of the time walking round the St Nicholas church and Union Terrace Gardens. The best section, for me, was walking down Patagonian Court and looking up at rear of Belmont Street, such a different angle that many people do not see. The new Revolution Restaurant has a lovely outside seating area that nestles perfectly into trees. The gardens were also looking great, but maybe I prefer this area due to my love of nature.

There was a great outcry when plans were made to build shops on the south side of Union Bridge, and when you see pictures of the flat-roofed, dreary building that was slotted into position, you can understand why people were not very satisfied with the result.

Even when I was a child I can remember walking past that building and thinking it was the ugliest in Union street. I cannot remember what shops it housed at the time, but I can certainly remember how awful I thought it looked. Looking at this site now I see a much brighter, happier building. The curved roof structures look like the billowing sails of a ship, and give shape to the unpractical and hideous roof. Colourful baskets of flowers which hang here and throughout the streets of central Aberdeen give life to the grey city on even the wettest of summer days.

The other day I was travelling on an overloaded double-decker bus at the end of a sunny day in the city. As we were struggling up Market Street memories of the voice of an elderly neighbour came into my mind. He told me of the horses that used to be kept at the bottom of the road. 'If the cart was too heavy, they used to just hitch another horse on.' I felt we could have done with another horse as the smoky, rattling engine hauled us up the hill. I often try to block out all the noise as I walk round the back of Marks & Spencer and know that the Wallace or Benholm tower that used to proudly stand there is now sitting in Seaton park, I wonder if any have even heard its name.

West towards Holburn Street, I took some photos of churches and prominent buildings. I could quite easily have spent much longer in this area, but it was getting late and I still had to walk to Old Aberdeen.

How many beautiful buildings do we warrant the right to demolish? The new buildings can look modern, but remain equally as grand, so what are we losing when we knock down one building to replace it with another? To achieve Aberdeen's architectural aspect in the first half of the twentieth century inevitably older buildings would have to be swept away. Changes were necessary in the ever-expanding city. But what did we lose? Are old photographs and memories enough, or would we prefer to experience the past firsthand? When did it become a travesty to lose whole streets full of history? Was it when we stopped designing equally meritorious buildings to replace past achievements?

The city's heritage is out there if we care to take the time to look.

Kerry J. Morrison.

St Mary's Cathedral.